W9-BLW-628

HOW IN THE WORLD?

HOW IN THE WORLD?

PAUL BENJAMIN
Foreword by Donald A. McGavran

LINCOLN CHRISTIAN COLLEGE PRESS
Lincoln, Illinois 62656
1973

HOW IN THE WORLD?

Library of Congress Catalog Card No. 73-80780

DEDICATED

To my father, A. P. Benjamin (1894-1967)
—who yearned to see the Commission fulfilled.

"For the earth will be filled with the knowledge of the glory of the Lord, as the waters cover the sea" (Hab. 2:14).

CONTENTS

FOREWORD xi

PREFACE xv

I. THE UNFULFILLED COMMISSION 1
Discipling the Nations 1
The Christian Congregation 3
The Quality of Christian Life 4
The Concern for Quantity 6
Enlarging the Task Force 8
The Whole Creation 9

II. ANALYZING THE COMMUNITY 11
Creating an Awareness 11
A Geographical Analysis 12
A Sociological Analysis 15
A Demographic Analysis 17
A Religious Analysis 19
Summary 20

III. MAKING A WITNESS-SURVEY 22

    Where to Begin? 22

    The Witness Survey 24

    The Advance Preparation 27

    Utilizing the Information 29

    Other Ways of Questing 30

    Caution and Summary 32

IV. UNDERSTANDING THE
      UNCOMMITTED 33

    The Communications Gap 33

    Life in the World 35

    Frailty of the Human Race 37

    The Strength of the Gospel 39

    Power to Become or Reject 42

V. GUIDELINES FOR WITNESSING 43

    First Guideline: Talk About Yourself 43

    Second Guideline: Talk About Them ... 47

    Third Guideline: Talk About Christ 48

    Presenting the Golden Text 50

    Fourth Guideline: Talk About Commit-
    ment 53

    Fifth Guideline: Talk About the Future .. 55

VI. CALLED TO MINISTER 57

    The Crucial Stage 57

    The Maturing Process 59

    Families in Transition 60

    Moving into Ministry 63

    Equipped to Serve 65

    An Area of Ready Response 66

VII. EMPOWERED BY THE SPIRIT 68

    Power for the Task 68

    The Significance of Pentecost 69

    The Holy Spirit and Mission 70

    The Divine Presence 72

    Power in Personal Life 75

    The Vision of World Evangelization 77

    STUDY SECTION 79

    Topics for Discussion and Notes 80

    APPENDIX 95

    How to Conduct a School of Evangelism 95

    Census Sample Card 106

    REFERENCES AND COMMENTS 108

FOREWORD

It is becoming increasingly clear that if America is to survive, a much larger proportion of her citizens must become practicing Christians. This means both more Christians and a greater number of illumined, determined, born-again Christians. If one wants more cream, he must have more milk.

God is at work in the world, creating a juster, more kindly and peaceful social order. He works both inside and outside the Church. However, cordial acknowledgement of that fact and joy in the evidences of his beneficent rule wherever they appear should not blind us to the likelihood that God's will becomes far more operative in bands of Christians (churches) than in bands of non-Christians. It is reasonable to assume that God works more through men and women who consciously yield to His will, search the Bible for light, and pray for guidance, than He works through men and women who rebelliously follow their own wishes, desire to know nothing of God's revelation, and never pray to Him.

The best way to make America peaceful, just, honest and pure is to multiply the number of Christians who meet regularly around the Bible to seek God's will and give themselves to the vivifying influence of the Holy Spirit. Each new generation and every part of it must be converted and receive Christ for itself. The horrendous situation our daily papers proclaim is impressive evidence that the time for deliberate aggressive evangelism is short. We have today. Whether we shall have tomorrow is not known. **Now** is the accepted time. Evangelism should both increase the number of Christians in existing churches **and** multiply the number of churches.

How in the World? is a much needed book. It will give hundreds of churches opportunity to equip their members for effective evangelism. As Kennedy of Coral Ridge, Florida, has so well demonstrated, merely exhorting Christians to evangelize is not enough. They must be **trained to evangelize.** They must be given opportunities to see how it is done and where it can be done effectively. How in the world can I communicate Christ? is a legitimate question. How in the world can this church bring twice as many persons to a saving, liberating knowledge of Christ? How in the world could we plant two daughter-churches? is a question many churches should be asking. These all require an answer. I hope thousands of groups of Christians will study this book and think their way through their many opportunities to disciple neighbors and friends, and establish new congregations in every nook and cranny of this fair land.

Dr. Benjamin has put the Church in debt by bringing out the *American Church Growth Series* and especially this second volume. I commend it. Ministers and laymen will do their congregations a favor by studying it intensively and putting its suggestions into practive.

> Donald A. McGavran
> School of Missions
> Fuller Theological Seminary
> Pasadena, California
> May 1, 1973

PREFACE

An increasing number of Americans are showing their willingness to be used by God in bringing others to Christ. Many congregations are conducting their own School of Evangelism. Others are following the CARE-PROMISE idea (see appendix). Recent testimony from preaching ministers has shown as many as a third of the congregation stepping out when challenged with the call to become more active personal witnesses.

It has become my deepening conviction that there is a real need for a book whose major emphasis is upon answering the question of these people and ministers, "Now, what do I do?" I am aware of helpful studies in this area. Some of these are mentioned in the reference section. At the same time, the place still exists, I feel, for another book which offers Christians practical help with their personal witnessing.

The study of this book should not serve as a substitute for "on the field" training. The principles of *How in the World?* must be utilized if they are to be effective. Some congregations may want to study the chapter on "Guidelines to Witnessing" first. Callers for Christ can then begin their work immediately.

Christian Educators, today, are also asking for the type of study in the church which equips the membership for ministry in the kingdom. This book could be an elective study in the Sunday School for one quarter. Congregations with set patterns about Sunday School literature could use *How in the World?* as supplementary reading. Some time for discussion should be allowed along with the regular lesson.

This study may be faulted by some because it does not deal more specifically with contemporary American sub-cultures. I feel that many of these areas demand specialized treatment which the length of *How in the World?* forbids. It is true, however, that much of the methodology suggested in this book can be used in any type of society. Some adaptation, I believe, will need to be made in any congregational situation.

How in the World? is certainly not intended to encompass all the types of witness and ministry in the Christian faith. The gospel is many sided, bearing upon every aspect of human life. Christ's Great Commission, however, calls upon his people to communicate the gospel to every person in the world.

This book is a part of a projected *American Church Growth Series* in which I hope other important phases of evangelism can receive attention. The first study in the series, *The Growing Congregation* and its companion *Workbook/Study-Guide* have been well received. My correspondence indicates that it is helping hundreds of congregations to "think evangelistically." Hopefully, *How in the World?* will come at the next stage and furnish help in actually "doing" the work of evangelism.

Those who complete this course of study will probably become an important part of the witnessing efforts of the congregation. Following the principle of the **taught** teaching, they can be enlisted as the teachers and trainers of others.

Permission is granted to those who wish to reproduce the witness-survey card (p. 26). The care-promise card (p. 102) and the census card (p. 106) are already in public domain.

ACKNOWLEDGEMENTS

I express my gratitude to the members of the administration and staff of Lincoln Christian College and Seminary for their help with *How in the World?* Miss Martha Porter and Mrs. Deltron Donaldson typed the manuscript. Prof. John C. Ralls suggested many important stylistic changes. Chancellor Earl C. Hargrove contributed important changes in content. President L. H. Appel has added his encouragement all the way along. Dean Enos E. Dowling has been sympathetic toward the need for literature in the field of American Church Growth.

Others from the college and seminary who have contributed are: Mr. Verlin Parker, Mrs. Mercedes Norheim, and Mr. and Mrs. Joe Seggelke. My association with the Church Growth Department has been very close. Dr. Rondal B. Smith, Dr. Max Ward Randall, and Prof. Cyril C. Simkins are each esteemed colleagues of mine in departmental work.

Questions for this study were prepared by Mr. Kenneth L. Overdorf. Mr. Carl Moorhous and Dr. Joe Ellis worked thoroughly through the manuscript and pointed out improvements which should be made. Dr. R. A. Raedeke suggested the chapter on the Holy Spirit.

The ministry of writing is dependent upon the help of many. I am grateful to all who have contributed in any way.

I

THE UNFULFILLED COMMISSION

Discipling the Nations

One day on a hill overlooking Jerusalem, a small band of men listened intently while their beloved leader gave his final instructions. "You shall receive power when the Holy Spirit has come upon you: and you shall be my witnesses in Jerusalem and in all Judea and Samaria and to the end of the earth" (Acts 1:8). Then he was gone (Acts 1:9). The group lingered a while, scarcely able to comprehend all that was taking place, and then returned to the city. There they awaited the promised Power.

During the three years the disciples had spent with Jesus, his instructions about witnessing had been less inclusive. Before sending the twelve on a mission in Galilee, he reminded them to "go nowhere among the Gentiles, and enter no town of the Samaritans, but go rather to the lost sheep of the house of Israel" (Matt. 10:5). On some occasions, Jesus followed an

1

exclusive kind of ministry himself. When a Grecian mother begged Jesus to exorcise the demon in her daughter, he graphically reminded her of the primacy of his mission to the children of Israel (Mark 7:24-30).

Although Jesus fulfilled his ministry on earth primarily with the Jewish people, his statements indicate that he intended for the gospel to be preached without ethnic restrictions. While he was on a teaching mission in the towns and villages, he encountered the question, "Lord, will those who are saved be few?" The inquirer was evidently hoping for an affirmative reply. Jesus answered this exclusive attitude by referring to the time "when men will come from east and west, from north and south, and sit at table in the kingdom of God" (Luke 13:22-30; cf., Matt. 8:5-13).

After the prophecies regarding his death and resurrection had been fulfilled (Luke 24:27), Jesus instructed his followers to carry out his world-wide evangelistic strategy. In Galilee, he said, "Go therefore and make disciples of all nations, baptizing them in the name of the Father and of the Son and of the Holy Spirit, teaching them to observe all that I have commanded you: and lo, I am with you always, to the close of the age" (Matt. 28:18-20).

Thus, with the restrictions upon witnessing lifted, the glad good news could be preached to everyone. Jesus had come, not only as the promised Jewish Messiah, but also as the Savior of all who put their trust in him (John 3:16). Beginning in Jerusalem, that wonderful news must be carried to the ends of the earth (Luke 24:47).

The Christian Congregation

How could a world-wide commission be carried out by only a handful of believers? The logistics alone of preaching the gospel to everyone are simply overwhelming. Other problems faced the early disciples. Their leader had been badly received by his own people (John 1:11). He died as a criminal. His followers were mostly from the lower classes in Jewish society. One of them had even been a tax-collector for the Romans. Their education was unaccredited (Acts 4:13). How could such a group possibly hope to start a world-wide movement? No one would pay attention to them.

It was the genius of the gospel to start spontaneously Christian congregations all around the Mediterranean. Later, Paul and his helpers systematically planted congregations in key cities of the Roman empire. As the disciples of Christ fanned out across that ancient world (sometimes because of persecution), they preached the good news of Jesus. Soon thousands upon thousands were confessing that Jesus Christ is Lord. Because of their methods of witnessing, in a few years Christianity had gained such momentum it attracted the attention of Rome itself.

Wherever the faith spread, the believers would gather periodically to gain instruction and find mutual encouragement through one another. They met where they could. Their places of worship included private homes (Rom. 16:5), three-storied buildings (Acts 20:9), and sometimes a beach (Acts 21:5).

The Christians who met in these new congregations were not content to keep the faith to themselves. They argued in the synagogues, they chattered to their friends, but they would not stop talking about Jesus Christ. Soon the whole community was talking. As one Christian lighted the candle of faith for another, he in turn lighted still another candle, and on and on the fire of faith spread. More and more were converted to the Way. Before long, an entire region had heard the gospel of Christ (Acts 19:10).

The Quality of Christian Life

The New Testament makes it clear that members of a congregation have a clear-cut responsibility to live lives acceptable to Christ. Paul is very unhappy about the sinfulness of the Gentiles and exclaims to the Ephesians, "You

4

did not so learn Christ!" Jesus Christ is both the head and the cornerstone of his church (Eph. 1:22; 2:20). The congregation belongs to Christ and must be constantly sensitive to his will. In addition, the church is also "built upon the foundation of the apostles and prophets" (Eph. 1:20).

Being sensitive to the will of Christ for a Christian includes the aim of continual spiritual development. The goal is the perfection of the heavenly Father (Matt. 5:48). Faith must be supplemented by virtue, knowledge, self-control, steadfastness, godliness, brotherly affection, and love (II Pet. 2:5-7).

The second "teach" of the Great Commission is a constant reminder that continued instruction for those already baptized is imperative. The work of nurture is an important task in any congregation. The young should receive spiritual help from those who are older. The very fact that congregations have "pastors" or "shepherds" points to the importance of caring for the sheep.

One of the reasons why the disciples made such inroads on a pagan world is because Christians were noted for the quality of their lives. Described by some writers as a "third race," the Roman world could not help but notice the way Christians supported one another in disease and sorrow. It was their hard-headed critics who were compelled to exclaim, "Look how they love one another!"

5

Yearning for this kind of high quality in the Christian life within the congregation has been one of the constant moving forces in the history of the church. Various movements in the American Church during the latter half of the twentieth century, and earlier, the Puritans of England, the Pietists of Germany, and the Quietists of France, all represented attempts by devout people to infuse the life of the church with greater Christian consistency. These groups simply could not find the quality they were looking for in many of the "organized" churches.

The efforts of a congregation to upgrade its own "body-life" must be constant and varied. A slack leadership usually results in a worldly membership. A lukewarm church is a disgrace to the Kingdom, however, Christ is constantly standing at the door, seeking readmission. Jesus re-enters the hearts of the people when they return to him in repentance and prayer (Rev. 3:14-22).

The Concern for Quantity

An emphasis upon quality in the congregation can often lead to a de-emphasis upon quantity. "We should take better care of the people we already have" is the usual rejoinder to a discussion emphasizing congregational outreach. Such an attitude is easily understood. No one

6

commends parents for bringing more children into the world if they are neglecting the ones already entrusted to their care.

By the same token, however, it could be strongly argued that the early Christians should never have departed from Jerusalem. Philip's successful preaching tour in Samaria was interrupted by the Spirit who prodded him into seeking a new convert who was traveling down the road to Gaza (Acts 8). Paul and Barnabas left a growing program of teaching and nurture in Antioch to pioneer in new fields for the Holy Spirit (Acts 13:1-3). The desire for quality, in the New Testament, never slackens the interest in quantity.

I am convinced that no congregation will become deeply involved in evangelism without a strongly determined effort. The reason is simple. Congregational concerns are usually on the side of input rather than outreach. It is easy for a preaching-minister to become the private chaplain to a few choice saints. Church members are usually happy to substitute committee meetings for calling. Worship has a way of constantly gaining the ascendency over witness. A spiritual re-awakening is often necessary before a congregation becomes concerned about the lost.

A study of church history points out the kind of major emphasis which nurture and teaching have received. It is well known that the leaders in the Reformation were so engrossed in reform, they had little time left for missionary concern. The "Great Century" in missions did not come until 300 years later. The absorbing concern for the church that is living, constantly diverts attention and energy away from the church that is not yet born.

Of course, no one can seriously suggest that Christ wants a slipshod church. On the other hand, what can Christians say to the disturbing fact that the majority of people on this globe have yet to be made aware of God's love for them through Jesus Christ? How can I go on, Sunday after Sunday, complacently singing missionary hymns, and not be disturbed by that fact? The resurgence of church growth, today, I believe is coming precisely at this point. Millions Christians are now deciding to become completely serious about the Great Commission. **Furthermore, a concern for quantity, it is often discovered, enhances rather than detracts from the quality of congregational life.**

Enlarging the Task Force

Only an enlarged labor force can possibly meet the demands of a greater task. Evangelism in the New Testament was never in the hands alone of a few paid professionals. The work of reaching others with the gospel belonged to the entire church. No staff can be delegated the responsibility of doing all the ministering for the congregation. Rather, those who are trained as leaders should have their primary responsibility in equipping others in the church for ministry (Eph. 4:11). Here is a place where American seminaries need to reevaluate their entire emphasis in professional training.

We can be thankful in our times that the New Testament doctrine of the ministry of all believers is gaining momentum every day. Some refer to this movement as the "laity phenomenon." Millions of Christians in the pews are looking beyond the concept of merely church-going. They are seeing themselves as willing ministers of Christ.

The Whole Creation

The command of Jesus Christ to "make disciples of all nations" was given nearly twenty centuries ago. In spite of the recent technological advances in communications, the world is still largely unevangelized. The masses without Christ must always be translated into individuals who live with "no hope and without God in the world" (Eph. 2:12). Plodding wearily through an earthly existence, they know nothing of the victorious hope which the gospel brings (John 10:10).

What does it mean to me that millions are "yet untold"? It means little, of course, if Christ is unimportant for my life. On the other hand, if I love him and his Word, then his concern becomes serious for me. I cannot erase the Great Commission from my New Testament. I can either fulfill it to the best of my ability or ignore it.

Many today have caught the vision of preaching "the gospel to the whole creation." They can never rest until "the earth will be filled with the knowledge of the glory of the Lord as the waters cover the sea" (Hab. 2:14). With constant awareness that the time is always short, they seek to bring the knowledge of God's redeeming love through Christ, to the whole world.

II

ANALYZING THE COMMUNITY

Creating an Awareness

Evangelism never takes place in a vacuum. The New Testament reveals an acute consciousness of the setting in which the gospel is being preached. The sermons recorded in the book of Acts indicate that the apostles were very concerned about the nature of their audience. Contrast, for example, the sermon of Peter on the day of Pentecost (Acts 2:14-22) with the sermon of Paul in Athens (Acts 17:16-21). Both men proclaimed the gospel of Christ. We find some striking differences, however, in the materials they cite to reach their audiences.

No congregation can afford to be unaware of the kind of community in which it functions. The term "pluralistic" is being increasingly used to describe American society. Communities differ greatly from on another. Contrasts in geographical setting, in sociological structure, and in religious backgrounds, soon become evident.

Many helps are available today to the congregation that wants to study its social setting. Every piece of information which furnishes insight regarding the nature of the community is valuable. Congregations should take a cue from the business world. Leaders in this field have already discovered the immense value of doing research for marketing.

A congregation can have its facts straight and still fail because it does not care enough for the people of a community. No amount of statistical information can compensate for a genuine interest in others. Concern coupled with information, however, makes a vital combination for the congregation interested in outreach.

A Geographical Analysis

This concern of a congregation can be projected geographically. Its boundaries should be charted on a map. The area may be sparsely or heavily populated. A river, freeway, railroad, cemetery, or an area of heavy industry sometimes provides a natural geographical boundary.

Various kinds of information are available to the congregation that wants to make a geographical analysis of an area. The local chamber of commerce is usually glad to share helpful materials. The U. S. Department of

Commerce, Census Bureau, Washington D. C., 20402, has geographical information on every state. Ask for pertinent materials for the area in which you are particularly interested. Also, check with real estate agencies for information.

For those interested in gathering geographical information in a rural area, a *County Atlas and Plat Book* gives the names of farm owners. It can be purchased from the office of the County Clerk or from a local farm organization. Also available is a more expensive book called *Annual Farm and Rents Directory.* In this volume, the name of the tenant as well as the landowner is supplied.

A congregation should determine its primary field and then proceed to work that area. It is self-defeating for the kingdom when a congregation tries to work a geographical area many miles from the church building and ignores families in the neighborhood. Some urban church planners suggest that a congregation work with a geographical area which has a three-mile radius. This radius can always be extended as the congregation grows. A congregation which tries to spread itself too thin may feel the frustration of much commotion and few results. In a less heavily populated area, however, a congregation can think in terms of a wider radius.

Various institutions may be located within the boundaries of an area which a congregation has determined to reach for the gospel. Perhaps a large university or a growing college may be found within the boundaries of primary concern. A huge retirement village or apartment complex could be on the drawing boards. Every institution within a geographical area of concern should be of special interest to the congregation.

A secondary geographical area may be a special interest also for a congregation. Perhaps adjacent to the area which the congregation intends to reach with the gospel is another section with large institutions. Within this territory, a military base, a government hospital, a migrant camp, or some other type of institution may call for the attention of the congregation. In order to keep its ministry concentrated enough, a congregation can decide to work a primary geographical area first and then turn to secondary areas. Geographical priorities can be established which enable a congregation to move in phases.

A map which shows the area of concern for a congregation is very useful. It can be prominently displayed in the church building as a visual aid. Attention should be called to it frequently. For reasons which are sometimes mysterious to those who do research in church growth, one section of a community may prove more receptive than another. A map indicating responses to the gospel will soon reveal the winnability of an area. For ease in mobility, an ink-spot-type of map rather than a pin-type is recommended.

A Sociological Analysis

Social groups make up the building blocks of any society. Individuals are the basic unit, of course, but every person is part of a web of social relationships.

In order to analyze the community socially, it is necessary to understand something of the groupings within the community. What religious affiliations, for example, predominate in the area? What kind of clubs does the community have and who belongs to them? Does the community have ethnic and racial minorities or majorities? How strong are these and are they growing or diminishing in strength? What is the political structure of the community? How strong is the influence of the public schools? Some communities are far more concerned about public education than others.

Closely tied in with social structure is economics. In fact, some sociologists look upon economics as being the heart of the sociological patterns of a community. People tend to form social groupings with those of their own economic level. Perhaps the quickest way of making a sociological survey of an area is by automobile. Drive across town on one street and back on the next until the entire area has been covered. The type of housing in the area is an immediate (but not final) index to a "lower-class," "middle-class," or "upper-class," status.

A subculture within an area of geographical concern may be viewed by the congregation as an opportunity or a threat. Through the rapid movement of social groups, particularly in urban areas, an entire community may be affected in a short time. A church building which has formerly been surrounded by middle-class whites may soon be the center of a growing black community.

When racial changes begin to take place, it is extremely important for the congregation to decide upon a course of action. The Great Commission is color-blind. Every effort should be made by the existing congregation to reach out to the people of every race. The former imposing church buildings which are now "faltering fortresses" are mute testimony to the failure of congregations to reach other cultures for Christ.

In changing neighborhoods, the existing church should deliberately start daughter-churches in the inflooding ethnic immigrants. The daughter-churches should be led by new ethnic Christians—deacons, elders, Sunday School teachers, and ministers. Then in due time, when the neighborhood has changed enough, the grand old church will be taken over by "Christians of our sort." Unless such daughter-churches are started, the grand old church will be taken over by "Christians definitely not of our sort," or by non-Christians for non-Christian ends.

A Demographic Analysis

Demography is statistical information about the characteristics of human populations. It includes their size and density, their growth, distribution and migration, as well as other factors relating to populations and social conditions.

Many sources of demographic information are available. A very handy reference, available in most bookstores is *The World Almanac* or *The American Almanac.* The U. S. Department of Commerce publishes a *Pocket Data Book* biennially. The demographic information in these sources is usually of a general nature.

A more specific source is also available through the U. S. Department of Commerce. It is a booklet for each state entitled *General Population Characteristics.* It includes the number of males and females as well as their age distribution in five-year increments. The use of this book should make it possible to construct a population pyramid of a given area. In the sample given below, see the preponderance of persons in age groupings from 5-14 and in the 35-44 brackets. Note also the small percentage of those whose ages range from 20-29.

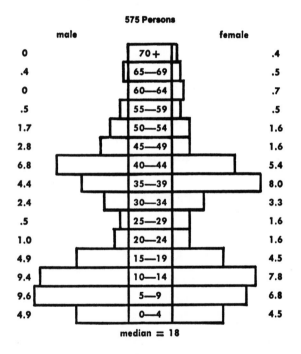

575 Persons

male	age	female
0	70+	.4
.4	65—69	.5
0	60—64	.7
.5	55—59	.5
1.7	50—54	1.6
2.8	45—49	1.6
6.8	40—44	5.4
4.4	35—39	8.0
2.4	30—34	3.3
.5	25—29	1.6
1.0	20—24	1.6
4.9	15—19	4.5
9.4	10—14	7.8
9.6	5—9	6.8
4.9	0—4	4.5

median = 18

A demographic analysis of a community may save a congregation from much mis-directed evangelistic effort. One congregation, in an attempt to reach the young people of its community, decided to erect a spacious educational plant. Later it discovered that a very small percentage of young people lived within its primary area of concern.

Rural areas often reflect a preponderance of the older people. Those of marriageable age have gravitated to urban areas in search of jobs or education. The suburbs usually have a high percentage of the middle aged with children still at home. A downtown apartment area may include a number of people whose families are reared as well as singles.

Utilizing information about population will help a congregation determine those areas where the greatest growth potential lies. Through the study of the comparative age groupings, it will also be able to decide on priorities and determine the type of thrust to be made first.

A Religious Analysis

No analysis of a community is complete without recognizing the influence of religion. The dominant religious influence in America is Christianity in a degree which is unparalleled in most countries of the world. For years European observers have been impressed by the pervasive influence of religion in American life.

"Religious pluralism" is the phrase frequently used by sociologists to describe the phenomenon made possible by the First

Amendment. Communities tend to be dominated by particular religious groups. Roman Catholics are prominent in many eastern cities and in Chicago. Lutherans, partly through the influence of immigration from Scandinavian countries, predominate in several northern states. Baptists have a strong influence in the South.

The predominating denomination often helps to influence the basic attitudes of a community. If a large religious group is strongly conservative, the entire community will have the tendency to be more traditional. Also, some denominations are more evangelistic than others. An area may be more open to the evangelistic endeavor of the congregation because such activity is a familiar part of community life. Others may be more resistant because they are inhabited predominately by religious groups who rely primarily on biological church growth rather than church growth through conversion.

Summary

Many congregations are failing to reach people in their communities for Christ, not because they do not care, but because they are unaware of the nature of the community. Jesus always spoke to the needs of every group because he understood them. Consequently, his words were always on target.

A church may be failing to reach a community with the gospel for several reasons. One of these reasons may be its failure to analyze the community properly. This chapter could provide an initial base for a congregation beginning deep research into its community situation.

The gospel is power. (Rom. 1:16-18) If it is not producing results in a given setting, the fault lies either with the people who are resisting it or with the Christians who are proclaiming it. If people are proving to be unwinnable, a community analysis may be the first step in finding out "why?"

III

MAKING A WITNESS-SURVEY

Where to Begin?

Assuming some kind of general analysis has been made of the community, what is the best way to find people who are living apart from the gospel? After many years of experience with this particular phase of evangelism, I am convinced there is no substitute for a house-to-house type of survey. Such a method is time honored. Reflecting on his experiences in the great metropolitan center of Ephesus, Paul cites his house-to-house type of ministry (Acts 20:20). On the university campus, one could speak of going from residence hall to residence hall, but the principle remains the same.

A house-to-house type of survey may present several problems. The difficulty in gaining access to certain kinds of apartment complexes is well known. Trailer courts often have restrictions about outside visitors. It may be necessary in some residential areas to get a permit from the city office before a religious survey is made. If a canvass of a particular area is being planned, it may be wise to inform the police department. They will be in a position to answer the inquiries of anyone who calls.

Sometimes the major problems are with the congregation. Some church members are reluctant to participate in any kind of religious survey. They feel it is an invasion of the other person's privacy. Others simply lack the nerve to approach a stranger. Many feel they do not have the time to help.

The fact still remains, however, that the concern of Christ which Christians are to demonstrate in the world requires information. The demands of love cannot be fulfilled without knowledge. In order to find those who need Christ and the ministry of the congregation, it is necessary to embark upon some kind of search-plan. The lost will not be found unless they are actively sought (Luke 15:1-10).

The place to begin is with the heart of every member of the congregation. How much do they really care about others? What does it mean to them that lives are being ruined daily by drug addiction, alcoholism, and sexual vice? How do they feel about the thousands who follow the hearse each day to the cemetery without hope? Do Christians really care about the millions of children growing up in North America with no religious instruction? Who will share the gospel with them? Every serious follower of Christ, I believe, must deal with these haunting questions.

If this chapter is being followed in some kind of group study, perhaps a frank expression of personal attitudes would be helpful. What can be done about the frightful neglect which the average congregation is constantly exhibiting toward those who need spiritual help? Individual and group prayer can sometimes do more to open up lives to the concern of God than anything else. Revivals have begun in countless communities because a few people began praying to the Lord of the harvest (Matt. 9:38).

The Witness-Survey

The idea of a community religious census has been a staple in North American evangelism for many decades. Yet, some are wondering today if a better method is available. The typical religious census presents some problems. Frequently, it lacks the personal touch. It sometimes represents a rather cool and statistical approach to people. Even more damaging is the idea that those outside the gospel are left with no word of Christian testimony. Neither does it allow any place for discussion between those who are already Christians.

Because of the deficiencies of the conventional religious census card, the idea of a community witness-survey is gaining attention. The basic information about the family is still gathered. The concept of further ministry is retained. But in addition, each surveyor is urged to include a personal testimony about Christ. A golden opportunity may be gone forever if the Christian is silent about his faith.

Study the sample questionnaire for a witness-survey. (See following page.) It is brief and yet helpful. The questions are arranged in the order which people feel most free to answer first.

Since some congregations may be reticent about launching out with a witness-survey, a conventional style census-card is included in the appendix.

In conducting a witness-survey, several fundamental rules should be kept in mind.

Rule One:

> Keep praying as you work. Remember the Presence (Matt. 28:20).

Rule Two:

> After ringing the doorbell (or knocking), stand where the person who is answering can see you with no difficulty.

Rule Three:

> Identify yourself and your calling companion(s) and state the purpose of your visit (see sample questionnaire).

WITNESS-SURVEY

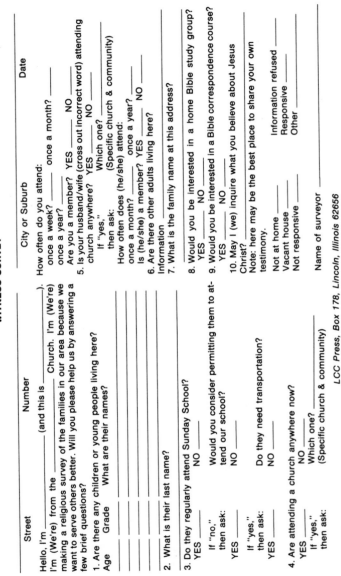

Street _____ Number _____ City or Suburb _____ Date _____

Hello, I'm _____ (and this is _____).
I'm (We're) from the _____ Church. I'm (We're) making a religious survey of the families in our area because we want to serve others better. Will you please help us by answering a few brief questions?

1. Are there any children or young people living here?
Age   Grade   What are their names?
_____
_____
_____
_____

2. What is their last name? _____

3. Do they regularly attend Sunday School?
YES _____ NO _____
If "no,"   Would you consider permitting them to at-
then ask: tend our school?
YES _____ NO _____
If "yes,"   Do they need transportation?
then ask:
YES _____ NO _____

4. Are they attending a church anywhere now?
YES _____ NO _____
If "yes,"   Which one? _____
then ask: (Specific church & community)

5. How often do you attend:
once a week? _____ once a month? _____
once a year? _____
Are you a member? YES _____ NO _____
5. Is your husband/wife (cross out incorrect word) attending
church anywhere? YES _____ NO _____
If "yes,"   Which one? _____
then ask: (Specific church & community)
How often does (he/she) attend:
once a month? _____ once a year? _____
Is (he/she) a member? YES _____ NO _____
6. Are there other adults living here? _____
Information
7. What is the family name at this address? _____

8. Would you be interested in a home Bible study group?
YES _____ NO _____
9. Would you be interested in a Bible correspondence course?
YES _____ NO _____
10. May I (we) inquire what you believe about Jesus Christ?
Note: here may be the best place to share your own testimony.

Not at home _____   Information refused _____
Vacant house _____   Responsive _____
Not responsive _____   Other _____

Name of surveyor _____

LCC Press, Box 178, Lincoln, Illinois 62656

Rule Four:

Do not act hurried. You may want to accept offered hospitality.

Rule Five:

Wherever possible, give a brief testimony about your personal salvation (i.e., "I have put my trust in Jesus Christ, Mr./Mrs. _____, and he means everything to me. I feel I must talk about him to others.") A genuine opportunity for further witnessing may develop through this testimony.

Rule Six:

Express your thanks for the interview.

Rule Seven:

Report **in writing** any information which may be helpful to subsequent callers.

Rule Eight:

Leave some printed material. Follow this rule regardless of whether or not people are home. Sign your name. Remember, it is illegal to put material in mailboxes.

The Advance Preparation

A knowledgeable chairman of a witness-survey can add immeasurably to the smoothness of the operation. Recruit callers well in advance. An alternate date should sometimes be set in case of inclement weather.

Daytime hours seem to work the best. Consequently, most congregations who have a number of working members must schedule their survey on a Saturday or Sunday afternoon.

It is not necessary that every caller have a partner. More territory, of course, can be covered if surveyors work alone. Many members of the congregation, however, will not canvass unless they have someone to help them. In order to secure their participation, a partner must be provided.

The chairman should have access to a detailed map of the area. "Fax" copies given to each surveyor can be extremely helpful. Outline with a marking pencil the exact territory which each witness is to cover. In suburbs with serpentine streets, this procedure can help minimize the instruction time.

A block plan can be utilized in some communities. Surveyors simply work around each block in an assigned area. Visitors are to cover every dwelling within a territory bordered by four streets.

The "no solicitor" signs may usually be ignored since you are not a solicitor—you are there to share Christ. You can check with people who are knowledgeable about the community, however, before deciding on a policy.

Utilizing the Information

The information which a church receives through a witness-survey is supremely important. Yet at no point is the average congregation more remiss than here. All too often, a congregation in a burst of evangelistic enthusiasm will survey a large area in the community. The reports are carefully tabulated and placed in the church files. Many months later, the unused information is still on record, becoming more dated every day. Meanwhile, many precious lives are being unreached.

Some researchers in church growth suggest the practical value of keeping double files. Cards are arranged (1) by street and address and (2) by the degree of responsiveness.

A visitor in the home cannot help but notice the physical surroundings of the family. Many North Americans are still stalked by poverty and disease. Children are often undernourished and unclothed. A large family may be straining its resources to the breaking point. Some homes will refuse any kind of material help. Others are happy to know that someone cares about their needs. Here is the place for Christians to practice what Jesus taught in Matthew twenty-five. The need in many families is unknown to members of a Christian community unless they care enough to find out.

Other Ways of Questing

The telephone survey has been used in many communities with favorable results. Some homes are inaccessible except by phone. Many of the larger cities have a telephone directory which lists all patrons by their address. Determine the area which is to be surveyed. Then make up a witness-survey card for each residence. Include the name of the subscriber, the address, and telephone number. Those who participate in the survey can be assigned responsibility according to streets.

The procedure is similar to the door-to-door witness-survey is programmed for a particular time. The telephone survey is not. Consequently, surveyors have more options in time. Also, it provides the possibility of participation by those who are not physically able to take part in a house-to-house survey. Many older Christians feel lonely and useless. Here is a marvelous opportunity for them to participate.

Smaller communities do not usually have a telephone directory listing subscribers by streets. Here it may be necessary to follow simply an alphabetical listing. In this case, the task of surveying may be divided up according to letters of the alphabet.

Some congregations have a time during the worship services when members are asked to make a list of individuals who need the ministry of the church. This procedure is valuable as an aid to the congregational quest. It also serves as a weekly reminder to the worshippers that the spiritual and physical needs of others must have a high priority for healthy congregational life.

Many churches are utilizing programmed transportation as an important way of questing for Christ. This method is particularly valuable in discovering children who need the gospel. It demands personnel who are extremely dedicated to their task.

Non-religious parents often place a high value on the moral influence of the church. Consequently, they will allow their children to receive Christian teaching. The congregation, however, must assume the responsibility for transportation. Experience teaches that children often furnish the door to the hearts of parents. The congregation must be constantly alert to that door of opportunity. Some major religious groups in America were at one time composed largely of children. These groups today are among the most rapidly growing fellowships in America.

Some congregations use a Christian "welcome-wagon" approach to newcomers in the community. Usually the ladies of the congregation are organized to visit every new family in the primary area of concern during the afternoon.

Caution and Summary

No congregational program of scheduled questing can compensate for the need of Christians to be spontaneous witnesses. As an illustration of the need to emphasize this kind of witnessing, I have heard of church members who see a new neighbor moving in. Next Sunday morning, they will contact their minister and ask him to make a call. The following Sunday they may even check to see if the minister has found the time. Meanwhile, they make no personal effort themselves to extend the ministry of the congregation. Christians should realize that they may be God's servant of the hour. There may be no other. On the streets, at the laundromat, in planes, they must go as Christ's ambassadors.

A programmed witness-survey is extremely valuable because it furnishes a systematic way of searching for those who need the gospel. Otherwise, many who may have become followers of Christ will never be contacted. Together with this type of scheduled evangelism is the all-important personal spontaneous witnessing by members of the congregation. Both methods, the scheduled and the spontaneous, are very valuable in questing for the precious lives of human beings.

IV

UNDERSTANDING THE UNCOMMITTED

The Communications Gap

Approximately three out of four persons living in North America are uncommitted to the Christian faith. The majority of these people have no active religious affiliation with a congregation. A broad gap in communications often exists between the Christian and the non-Christian. Sometimes a well-meaning member of a congregation can actually harm the cause of the gospel through his witnessing. He may lack awareness of the basic thought patterns of those who live outside the gospel.

Here is the place where the congregation can constantly utilize the input of its members who formerly lived in the world. No one knows more about the nightmare of alcoholism than a former alcoholic. A young divorcee with several children is well equipped to talk about the trauma of rearing a family in a fatherless home. A widower who has lost his companion of many years knows something about loneliness. The person who has been converted from materialism has experienced how empty a life of "things alone" can be.

These people can be resource personnel in the congregation which decides to care more about others. They can enlighten the whole church about particular areas of concern and how to meet these needs with the gospel. Moreover, they may be recruited in special categories as callers who deal specifically with those who have particular problems. Alcoholics Anonymous discovered this principle years ago. A faculty colleague of mine, whose leg had been amputated, called in hospitals on recent amputees. His purpose was to give encouragement and hope, while at the same time, to speak a good word for the gospel, the only source of eternal hope.

This chapter is written with the hope of giving Christians a better understanding of the uncommitted. Many Americans have grown up from the cradle roll in the Christian faith. They attended their first service of worship in the arms of their mother. Consequently, it is sometimes difficult for them to hold sympathetic attitudes toward those who have been reared with a different perspective. Devout Christians are often appalled because of the overt sinfulness of human beings. Shock sometimes turns into scorn.

Christians must realize, however, that it is illogical to expect the uncommitted to live according to Christian ethics. Here is a place where many Christians need to rethink their basic attitude. Jesus derided the hypocrites of his day, but he showed great tenderness toward those ensnared by sin (Luke 7:36-50). Consequently, he was ridiculed by his religious contemporaries who complained, "this man receives sinners and eats with them" (Luke 15:2). God is the one who will judge sinners. Our task is to evangelize.

Life in the World

The Bible makes a stark contrast between those who live for Christ and those who live in the world. The term "world" is often used in the scriptures to indicate those who live outside the Christian faith. The Christian lives "in the world" but he is not to be "of the world." The world in its present condition cannot receive the Spirit of truth which Jesus brings (John 14:17).

What are some characteristics of those in the world? With many, the pleasures of the body become very important. Paul is evidently verbalizing the attitude of the worldly Corinthians when he said, "Food is meant for the stomach and the stomach for food" (I Cor. 6:13). If an act brings enjoyment to the body, then according to the worldly philosophy, it is senseless to deny it. Money for the worldly person often becomes very significant since it is a means to provide added enjoyment for the body.

The Christian should realize that he may be talking to an individual who is deeply committed to the world. The sinner, until he repents, is not interested in a way of life which emphasizes self-control. His pleasure revolves around the uncontrolled desires of his body. Little is forbidden to him, provided he can escape an earthly penalty.

One must not assume, however, that all worldly individuals are devoted to physical pleasure. Many Americans live highly moral lives apart from any religious faith. They accept much of the ethical teaching of the Christian faith, but they reject belief in a supernatural God and consequently, the idea that Christ is the divine Son of God.

Many Americans have been educated from a purely rationalistic viewpoint. All supernaturalism has been ruled out. The emphasis in their education has been on the self-sufficiency of man. A student may have uncritically accepted the rationalistic presuppositions of his professors. Consequently, he is not open to the complete claims of the gospel, especially the idea of dependence upon another Being.

Too often in the past, Christians have turned aside from those who disbelieved the Biblical claims about Christ. Unlike the early Christians, they have been unwilling or unable to give a reason for their faith (I Pet. 3:15). The doubting person who speaks of his unbelief in regard to the Christian faith may be more open to the gospel than he lets on to a Christian. He may have come to the place in his life where he is beginning to doubt his doubts. As a witness to Christ, you may be coming to him at just the right time.

The average non-Christian American, however, is probably not addicted to the flesh or troubled by intellectual doubt. European writers for years have pointed to the pervasive influence of religion in American culture. The uncommitted person in America is most frequently simply complacent about the gospel. What he needs is an opportunity to hear the gospel from the lips of a dedicated believer. He must also be shown what it means for Christians to love others. The growth patterns of evangelistic congregations in North America provide ample evidence of the openness of our society to Jesus Christ.

Frailty of the Human Race

Any effort to understand some of the basic attitudes of the uncommitted leads into the deeper question of the nature of human beings. The Psalmist inquired, "What is man?" That question has continued to occupy the attention of leading thinkers across the centuries.

Although man has been crowned by God "with glory and honor" (Psalms 8:5), the signs of his frailty are unmistakable. His "days are like grass" and he is soon gone "like a flower of the field" when "the wind passes over it" (Psalms 103:15-16). His life may be compared to the early morning mist which quickly vanished before the rising sun (James 4:14). Contrasted to the splendor of the moon and the stars, the Psalmist is amazed that God has any concern for man (Psalms 8:3-4).

As Tennyson observed in *In Memoriam,* "Thou madest man, he knows not why, He thinks he was not made to die." Yet as everyone knows, we all must die. Each day brings us a step closer to our own funeral.

In addition to the certainty of death, life is made more weary because of human sinfulness. No computer can calculate the bitterness suffered by the human race because of wickedness. The Christian should spare himself any envy of those who lead lives of unrighteousness. Pay-day is always someday! The narrow gate of righteousness may be difficult to find, but it leads to life. The broad way to sin always leads to self-destruction (Matt. 7:13-14).

Man's frailty is further accented by his need for other humans. The idea of the strong man who "makes it" in life without human love is a myth. Human personality can only become truly human in a community of other persons. When deprived of the affirmation which comes from others, man usually becomes despondent.

The strength of man can never be celebrated without an acute consciousness of his frailty. The uncommitted also share in the basic weakness of the human race. No amount of self-deception can eradicate the presence of the crippling forces which are able to devastate man. It is important that the Christian witness be consciously aware of the basic human situation.

The Strength of the Gospel

The gospel has tremendous power because it touches man at his point of greatest weakness, Death remains a mystery which human intellect cannot unravel. The writings of philosophers cancel out each other when they attempt to probe the silence of the tomb. Their conjectures add little satisfaction to the quest of the hjman heart. The situation is little different with other religions. Only Christianity can present the teachings of a resurrected Savior.

The uncommitted person has no real solution to the problem of death. He may be convinced that life has no separate existence apart from the body. Consequently, the grave ends all. Perhaps he is postponing any thoughts of death by throwing all his energies into living now. The point is however, that he has no real answer.

The solution to the riddle of death is squarely met by the gospel. Only Jesus Christ the Savior has "abolished death and brought life and immortality to light" (II Tim. 1:10). It was no happenstance that the resurrection of Christ was central in the preaching of the early Christians. The raising of Jesus from the grave was the irrefutable evidence of God's victory over the sting of death (I Cor. 15:55).

Christians seek to share with the uncommitted the knowledge that life on earth is a brief pilgrimage. Human beings are transients on a spinning globe. For those who believe in Christ, the life beyond is in the Father's house (John 14:1). Death need not be a defeat for anyone who through faith claims the promises of the Savior.

The strength of the gospel also comes at the point of man's guilt and his need for forgiveness. The non-Christian is often unaware that the church is composed of forgiven sinners. Consequently, he may try to point with pride to his own goodness. He must be shown that no person can claim righteousness on his own before a perfect God. "All have sinned and fall short of the glory of God," the scripture affirms

(Rom. 3:23). Salvation can never be merited. It is the gift which God gives to those who claim Jesus Christ as Savior" (Eph. 2:8).

Often the sins of the uncommitted have become an unbearable burden to him. He is not trying to make excuses for himself: he is honestly looking for help. Here is the place where the witness can echo the saying of the early Christians, "Christ Jesus came into the world to save sinners" (I Tim. 1:14).

The need which human beings have for an affirming relationship with others is also met by the gospel. Modern society with its rapid urbanization imposes a terrible burden of loneliness upon many people. The person who moves from the small community to the city often experiences the excitement of personal freedom. Prying eyes have been left behind. But being anonymous also carries with it the double edge of not belonging anywhere. "I could die tomorrow," a city dweller says, "and no one would even notice."

The idea of the congregation was divinely given to help in meeting the basic need of humans for a positive association with others. It is important for Christians to find encouragement through other Christians (Heb. 10:25). God did not intend for his new Israel to face a hostile world alone.

Those who are now uncommitted to the gospel have sometimes had a negative experience with a previous congregation. They may be unaware that congregations differ in their basic attitudes. Emphasize the idea with them that all congregations should not be judged by some. Meanwhile, the point needs to be strongly made, that Christians should provide an affirming experience for each other.

Power to Become or Reject

The Christian witness is constantly dealing in "futures." The uncommitted person to whom he is speaking has all the potential of greatness in the kingdom. God can lift up every individual who comes to him through Jesus Christ (John 1:12). No matter what the past has been, a new future can begin now. The Christian yearns for the uncommitted to find new life in Christ. He shares the compassion of Jesus for those who are "harassed and helpless, like sheep without a shepherd" (Matt. 9:36).

The tremendous concern of the Christian must never lead him to the denial of human freedom. Man is free not to choose God. The Christian is a witness to the power of God in the scriptures and in his own life. He can present all the reasons why everyone in the world should turn to Christ. Yet, in this life, God grants the uncommitted the freedom to remain uncommitted.

42

V
GUIDELINES FOR WITNESSING
Finding Some Conversational Hooks

Many Christians have a very deep concern for others in their community who are without the gospel. Still, they are reluctant to speak to them about Christ. Why? Much of this reticence, I am convinced, is based upon the inadequacy-fear syndrome. They think their witnessing is inadequate and they fear the response they might receive if they try.

The experience of thousands who are witnessing today indicates that the inadequacy-fear-syndrome is not usually a real threat. Most Christians are far more effective witnesses than they realize. Furthermore, they find that their fears regarding an anticipated negative response are usually ungrounded.

This chapter is devoted to a discussion of some guidelines for witnessing. The word "guidelines" has been chosen because it is virtually impossible to cover all the facets of witnessing in detail. Personalities and circumstances are too varied. A Christian may be working in an American sub-culture which may require a special kind of awareness on the part of the witness. The sociological background which I have in mind is primarily a settled-community type of evangelism. The same basic guidelines, however, are applicable in a variety of situations.

The following suggestions provide a plan of thinking for the Christian witness. Most successful witnesses have some type of mental format which they follow in leading others to Christ. By memorizing each guideline in this chapter, you can have some "hooks" on which to hang your conversation. The WITNESSING TRIANGLE below furnishes a visual aid:

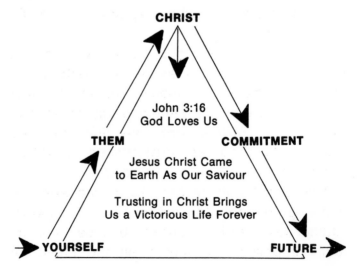

CHRIST

John 3:16
God Loves Us

THEM

COMMITMENT

Jesus Christ Came
to Earth As Our Saviour

Trusting in Christ Brings
Us a Victorious Life Forever

YOURSELF

FUTURE

The fright of not knowing what to say can be overcome by memorizing these guidelines. These need not be adhered to slavishly in such a way as to become mechanical. They simply become the theme upon which the witness can do his own improvizing. Experience is always the best teacher. A witness becomes more confident as he continues witnessing.

The New Testament should be kept clearly in mind when you are leading another person to Christ. It is the basic authority in the Christian faith. The Acts of the Apostles is an especially important book for the witness. It is the record of the way the apostles and others carried out the announcement of Jesus "that repentance and forgiveness of sins should be preached in his name to all nations, beginning from Jerusalem" (Luke 24:47-52).

There are numerous instances of people who came to Christ recorded in Acts. These accounts should be carefully studied. On the day of Pentecost, over 3000 were baptized (Acts 2:41). Sometimes an entire household responded to Christ (Acts 16:31). In other instances, an individual became a Christian (Acts 8:35-38). The following guidelines are taken primarily from these accounts of conversion in the book of Acts. Additional references to these case-studies in conversion will be mentioned in the latter part of this chapter.

First Guideline: Talk About Yourself

Identification is usually the first step in approaching another person with the gospel. On the day of Pentecost, Peter hastened to respond to the misapprehension which some of the people had about the apostles (Acts 2:14-15).

If two witnesses (or sometimes three) are working together, the most logical identification would be the congregation with whom they are associated. The leader can easily say at the door, "Mr. _____ and I are visiting (tonight) in the name of Christ. We are from (name the congregation). May we come in for a few minutes?"

Since this type of calling is often done in the evenings, the fear factor in modern society makes it imperative that the witnesses establish their identity as quickly as possible. An identification badge may be helpful. Sometimes a telephone call prior to the visit may be necessary to establish contact.

Assuming the witnesses have gained entrance to the dwelling, they may spend the next few minutes giving additional information about themselves. This step is important in establishing rapport. It will help the interview if the family being visited sees the callers in the context of their occupation and personal background. Sometimes a little good-natured humor at this point helps to relax the atmosphere.

Second Guideline: Talk About Them

It is very important that the witnesses learn about the family on whom they are calling. (This family could be referred to as the "callees"—a good word which I seldom see.) People are not interested in becoming a percentile point on a church-growth graph. They want to be treated with the special concern which rightly belongs to every human being.

The callers may already have some basic information about the callees as a result of a previous witness-survey. This knowledge should be firmly implanted in the minds of the witnesses. It can serve as the springboard for the conversation. Many topics such as vocation, family, religious heritage, can be discussed in a general way.

Although the callers must avoid prying into the personal lives of the callees, frequently a friendly visit by a concerned Christian will open up the well-springs of a distressed life. People are often lonely and troubled. They will reveal their troubles many times to a sympathetic visitor. Because they are ambassadors for Christ, the witnesses will want to listen carefully.

If a family is cold or hungry, a Christian will immediately take steps to alleviate the need (Matt. 25).

It is possible that talking about "them" will take up the entire evening. The other calls on the list must be postponed. It is amazing how people will turn to those who genuinely care for them. As a Christian witness, your very presence in another home which brings you no favor, financial or otherwise, is a silent testimony to your concern.

If the witnesses find out that the callees are not responding favorably to their visit, then they should abbreviate their call. The gospel is not to be forced on anyone; rather it is to be offered to all. The family being visited may have some very good reaasons why **at this particular time,** they are not interested in talking. Their brevity should not always be regarded as unfriendliness.

Third Guideline: Talk About Christ

The early Christians were constantly talking to others about Christ. "We cannot but speak," they said, "of what we have seen and heard" (Acts 4:19). Assuming that the callees are favorable to the witnesses, then the next guideline is to "talk about Christ."

Witnessing to Christ is the apex of the gospel presentation. In the instances of conversion cited earlier in this chapter, the dominant theme was the person of Jesus (Acts 2:22-36; 8:34-35; 16:31-32). The act of witnessing, in essence, is simply one Christian telling someone else about Christ. According to the writer of Hebrews, Jesus is God's last word (1:1). The glad news of the gospel across the centuries has been that "God was in Christ reconciling the world to himself" (II Cor. 5:19).

It is falsely assumed by some church-people that everyone in America has already heard the gospel. "Look at the number of sermons on radio and TV every week," they say. This kind of misconception can be easily dispelled by personally visiting with Americans about Christ. The depth of ignorance is often tragic. Many university students are unable to speak about Christ in an intelligent way. They have never read the Bible. It is not just overseas where people need to learn about Christ. People are also languishing in this country because they know nothing about the word of God (Hos. 4:6).

In sharing the gospel with others, many Christians also overlook the importance of the Bible. "The word of God is living and active" (Heb. 4:12). It is a matter of record that thousands have been led to Christ through reading the Bible. A Christian witness needs to stand behind the word of God and allow its power to work.

Presenting the Golden Text

There are good reasons why John 3:16 is quoted more than any other verse in the Bible. No other scripture states more beautifully the heart of the gospel. The Who-What-Why-When-Where-How of the Christian message can be found in this wonderful verse. I know the dean of a seminary who never preaches a sermon without quoting John 3:16.

You can lead into a conversation about Christ by reading or quoting The Golden Text and then asking, "Mr. and Mrs. _____, would you mind telling us what you think about this scripture?" Callers are frequently remiss at this crucial juncture because they do not give the callees enough time to answer. Sometimes waiting seems terribly long.

When the callees do respond, listen very carefully to what they are saying. It has been rightly said that to miss the other person's point of view is to miss the person himself.

As the discussion continues, the entire conversation can revolve around the central themes of the Golden Text. These main ideas can be stated as follows:

God Loves Us.
Jesus Christ Came to Earth As Our Savior.
Trusting in Christ Brings Us a Victorious Life Forever.

It may be necessary to refer to The Golden Text again and again with its emphasis upon **God, Christ,** and **Man.** Remember to let the scripture work. People are not converted to Christ merely through human ability; they come to him through the witness of the Word and the power of the Holy Spirit. The basic Christian truth of John 8:6 is amplified in the following box. Read over this section repeatedly.

GOD LOVES US

The uncommitted may need to be told repeatedly that God loves them. Unforgiven sin brings with it a feeling of estrangement between the uncommitted and God. God bridges that barrier by holding out loving arms to all those who will return to him (Luke 15:11-24).

JESUS CHRIST CAME TO EARTH AS OUR SAVIOR

The unmistakable evidence of God's love is the fact he sent Jesus Christ into the world as our Savior. Man left to his own devices has always lost his way. The wicked powers which surround him constantly lure him to his own destruction.   Only God could provide the solution to man's wretchedness. Jesus came as the "Savior" to redeem man and show him the way.

> ### TRUSTING IN CHRIST BRINGS US
> ### A VICTORIOUS LIFE FOREVER
>
> "Eternal life" is not just a reference to the future; it also includes the quality of life now. Life for the Christian takes on a totally new dimension. And yet, our current trust in him will not be betrayed at the grave. "Shall not perish" is not an idle promise; it is the firm assurance which comes because Jesus Christ won the victory over the grave (John 14:19).
>
> It should be pointed out to the non-Christian that the Christ never promises us a life without problems. He does assure us that we shall not live without hope.

The chances are that in an American situation, the callees already believe in the reliability of the Christian Scriptures. If they are in doubt at this point, it may be necessary to approach them differently. Consult the reference section for special help with this problem.

Fourth Guideline: Talk About Commitment

If the callees acknowledge The Golden Text as a valid truth-claim about Jesus Christ, then they must decide whether they will yield their lives to him. It may come very naturally to ask, "Mr. and Mrs. _____, are you willing to trust Christ completely and follow him?" One member of the family may be more responsive than another. An older child often shows far more willingness to trust Christ than his parents.

Now may be the time to utilize case studies from the book of Acts and point to those who made their first-time decisions for Christ. The conversion of the 3000 on the day of Pentecost could furnish a good starting place to begin reading. Those who formerly rejected Christ were now turning to him in repentance. The apostle Peter instructed them in their response (Acts 2:37-42).

Another account of a first-time decision for Christ is the record of an Ethiopian. When Philip found him on the road to Gaza traveling in his chariot, he was reading from Isaiah. Philip joined him in his chariot and "told him the good news of Jesus" (Acts 8:35). The Ethiopian was baptized and continued on his way rejoicing (Acts 8:36-39). The conversion of the Philippian jailor along with all his family is still another account of commitment to Christ (Acts 16:25-34). You may also want to include other references from the New Testament.

Perhaps the callees were formerly active with a Christian congregation. The years have eroded a previous commitment. Their relationship may have been horizontally with church people, but not vertically with Christ. The congregation may have failed to nurture their reed-like faith. Although they have come to a new awareness of their need for Christ, they may want to make a re-commitment of their lives.

Do not try to rush the callees into a decision. At the same time, however, point out the perils of putting off decision. Indicate that continued procrastination is ultimately a rejection of the gospel.

The affirmative response of the callee should be the cause for great rejoicing. The callers should not refrain from showing their happiness. It may seem very natural for the witnesses to lead the group in prayer. Encourage those who have made a commitment to pray also.

If the response of the callees is negative, the witnesses must be careful not to show a thwarted or depressed attitude. The tendency sometimes is for the callers to blame themselves for failure. They feel conscious of mistakes in their presentation. The worst mistake of all is to quit trying. Even Jesus failed with some. Keep in mind the idea that the word of God works in a mysterious way. One never knows when or how a seed takes root (Mark 4:26-29).

Dwight Moody was often criticized for his evangelistic methods. He always said, though, that he liked the way he was doing it rather than the way his critics were not doing it.

Fifth Guideline: Talk About the Future

The gospel is involved with a person's total future, but it is not mere pie-in-the-sky-ism. The future begins now. Commitment to Christ is the fork in our personal road.

Christ must be given an opportunity to grow in our lives. Christians cannot develop properly without prayer and the word. Contact with God through his word and prayer will produce in the Christian its beneficial effects upon his actions in the business world, in education, in family and recreational life as well as all other social relationships. Those who make a decision for Christ should be encouraged to spend a part of each day in private devotions (Matt. 6:6). Make certain every home has a copy of the New Testament, preferably in a modern translation.

The future of the committed must include others who are Christians (see also the next chapter). Nowhere in the New Testament do we find a strictly solo kind of Christianity. Growth in Christ depends in a large way upon the quality of our fellowship with other believers. In most situations, it is natural for those making decisions for Christ to fellowship with the people

who sought them. Finding a happy congregational home should be a joyous experience for those who are now committed to
follow Christ.

The person committed to Christ lives a
different type of life from the worldling. No person shall see God whose heart continues to remain impure (Matt. 5:8). The future must include
turning away from the habit of sin. At the same
time, it includes turning to right activities. His actions will become increasingly beneficial to
everyone.

Physical death for the Christian is not the
end—only a new kind of beginning. The future
for those committed to Christ includes life
forever with the Father. The gift of a new future
is given by God to all those who are trusting in
Jesus Christ and continually obedient to his will.

VI
CALLED TO MINISTER
The Crucial Stage

The new Christian should not be pessimistic about his early failures in the Christian life. Jesus faced some of his greatest temptations immediately after his baptism (Matt. 4:1-11). His hearing the voice of God acknowledging him to be his Son and the coming of the Spirit upon him became the occasion for an immediate attack by the devil. Similarly, any person who commits himself to the divine will must undergo the constant harassment of demonic forces.

In the book of Hebrews, the writer says of Jesus, "He learned obedience through what he suffered" (Heb. 5:8). The victorious life in Christ does not cancel out the possibility of dark days. Even these times, however, can enrich the Christian life if they are accepted with a proper attitude.

The first few months in the life of a Christian are the time of greatest need for the warm concern of other Christians. The one who has committed his life to Christ may be barely standing up spiritually. He needs a great deal of help.

Many churches have a special class constantly in progress for new people (which may include those who have not committed themselves to Christ, but are thinking about it). This class should provide a genuine sharing experience for those who are just starting (or beginning again) in the Christian life. The teacher should be one of the most sensitive Christians in the entire congregation. Many of the friends which new Christians will make in the congregation will probably be from this class. Such a class will make it easier for the new Christian to relate to the total congregation. The procedure of having such a class is very important for a large congregation.

What are some basic experiences which are important in the life of the newly committed? First of all, they should learn to pray. They also need to learn how to use the Bible. A Biblical outline-type of study is extremely valuable for them. They should be given basic information about the church and the Christian life. Christian stewardship is another important topic, as is the value of Christian worship. Another area, often neglected, is Christian witnessing. New

Christians, because they have just come from the world, often make the most enthusiastic witnesses. With encouragement and training, they can soon be leading others to Christ.

The Maturing Process

The writer of Hebrews was deeply distrubed because the Christians to whom he was writing had failed to move beyond the "elementary doctrines of Christ." He pleaded with them to "go on to maturity" and reminded them of a goal. These "sluggish" Christians are to imitate men like Abraham and go on to "the full assurance of hope" (Heb. 6).

It is very important for preaching-ministers and other spiritual leaders in a congregation to examine the kind of goals which they have for people. In many churches, the goal becomes the attendance at a certain number of worship services and the giving of a stated amount of money. Those who reach these "checkpoints" are the ones who have spiritually arrived and often become the congregational leaders.

The problem with the "checkpoint" system is its failure to recognize the Christian life in its totality. Those who arrive at the tithe of their net income are not challenged to proceed beyond that checkpoint. The attendance at a certain number of worship services becomes a substitute for a genuine practice of the Christian stewardship of time.

Many congregations provide a kind of lockstep for their membership. The idea of Christian freedom, so precious in Galatians and other New Testament books, is lost in a new kind of traditionalism (Gal. 5:1). The greatest congregations are those where the leadership is constantly encouraging individual initiative. This kind of freedom is always at the heart of growth in the kingdom. It is flexibility rather than regimentation which is the key to individual members' developing at their own pace. Otherwise, it is difficult for any person to rise spiritually above the level of the group.

Families in Transition

Americans are among the most mobile people in the world. Approximately one in five persons moves every year. This kind of mobility has been a great concern to church leaders for a number of years. People are frequently lost to the Kingdom during a time of transition. At the community level, congregational leaders are often completely perplexed by the response which they receive when calling upon people who have formerly been active in a congregation.

The patter is usually along the following lines. It has come to the attention of leaders in an urban congregation that a family of their religious group is moving into the area. The people of the congregation call in the home. They invite the new family to worship with them. The callers are nonplussed because of the evasive response of the newly arrived family. "What is taking place here?" the callers wonder.

The new family in the community, who have been active in a former congregation, may have been involved in a highly regimented situation. Perhaps the husband has served on the church board. His wife may have been a leader in one of the women's circles. They consequently found themselves totally immersed in congregational activities. Later, they may resent the constant pressures upon them to attend meetings, but they do not know how to escape. A move to a new territory provides them with the outlet.

The chances are that these people who have served faithfully in a congregation somewhere else have not turned their back on the gospel. They are not pagans. What they want is the opportunity to take a fresh look at their entire religious situation. Christian parents may feel they have neglected family life. Perhaps they have children who have gone astray even though the father and mother were very active in "church work."

If they are retired people, it may be their opinion that one retires from the church just as he retires from any other institution. If they are young people, their concern may be for a place to worship which is less formal than the one from which they came.

All Christians need a group of believers to whom they can relate on a primary basis. Families in transition are no exception. The new family in the community is probably trying to make some adjustments. They may want to avoid a congregational-lockstep situation from which they have just come. Their spiritual life, of course, can become precarious unless Christian influences in their life are continued.

New families in the community should be treated with great sensitivity. They should be loved for themselves and not because they may help increase the attendance and offerings for the church. If they have been congregational leaders in the past, they may want to serve in a different way.

It may be that a couple who become new members of a congregation can be attracted by the idea of being missionaries to some particular age group in a community. This responsibility then becomes their primary one and they are allowed to exercise it with flexibility. They are encouraged to use their own creative abilities rather than follow a prescribed set of institutional rules. Many people who are holding off a congregation at arm's length will respond if they are properly approached.

Moving into Ministry

The consideration above has been for those who have been worn out in a previous congregational experience through hyper-activity. On the other hand, one of the great tragedies in the history of the church is the kind of passive role which people in the pews have usually assumed. Often the periods of great revival in Christianity have come when these people have become religiously awakened. The New Testament clearly teaches the ministry of all believers (see my discussion on this subject in *The Growing Congregation*). Only as that doctrine moves from a theory in the congregation and becomes a part of practice can there be any hope of a world-wide spiritual revolution.

Pulpit-ministers in the congregation seem to have an increasing difficulty in understanding their own role. For many years, the American ministry has been educated from the viewpoint of a clergy-laity perspective. Within that framework, the seminarian becomes "the" minister of a congregation. His task is to minister for the congregation who provide his physical livelihood. Many congregations are also having difficulty in making adjustment to the fact that the contemporary minister cannot do everything people are demanding of him. They often want to become critical of their minister who is not living up to their constant expectations.

Changes are seldom made in the life of the church without tension. If the American church can be guided through the present time of adjustment in the clergy-laity situation, the new opportunities for Christianity are limitless. Patience on the part of everyone who is concerned must be required. Those who can see the future are often to be faulted because of their insensitivity to the present.

The Sunday morning worship service of the congregation should be looked upon as a meeting of the ministers of the church. Every Christian is a minister of Jesus Christ (I Pet. 2:4-10). Since everyone cannot lead at once, some of the ministers are designated to lead in worship. Christian gifts vary. Some may have musical accomplishments. Others like that unknown person in the New Testament may be famous for preaching the gospel (II Cor. 8:18). Each minister should use his abilities "for building up the body of Christ" (Eph. 4:12). No member of the group should look upon his contribution as inferior to others (I Cor. 12:14-26).

Equipped to Serve

It is not right to expect members of the congregation to become ministers of Christ without obtaining help. Colleges and seminaries devoted to educating full-time workers in the church have been in existence for centuries. These have functioned primarily for the clergy. With the emphasis of our times upon the importance of people in the pew has come the desire to equip them for ministry.

Some theological schools are making deliberate efforts to provide training for the laity. Often a basic problem stems from the attitude of the people in the congregation who have never been taught to regard themselves as ministers. They can only view classes being offered in the area of counseling, witnessing, teaching, pastoring, and biblical study as being related to a clergy.

Another problem comes from those who now function as clergy. The idea of training laymen for ministry often brings about a basic reorientation in attitude for the pulpit-minister. He has looked upon himself as one whose basic role was to minister to others instead of teaching others to minister.

In communities where the New Testament concept of the ministry of all believers has been accepted, some congregations are pooling their leadership resources in mini-type colleges. A pulpit-minister whose major was in counseling offers courses to laymen in that area. Another church leader specializes in helping Christians share their faith with others. Since American church buildings are among the most expensive and least-used pieces of real estate in the world, space for classes is usually no problem. The primary goal of the entire operation is not to produce "minor-clergy," but to help the people of God become genuine ministers throughout the everyday experiences of life. Service to Christ can be viewed in its totality rather than creating a false division between the "sacred" and "profane."

An Area of Ready Response

The new members in the congregation are frequently the ones who are most eager to step out into new adventures of service. They will often witness to their faith when older members will not. Sometimes their willingness to serve creates problems. Older members feel they are being bypassed as the new members rise in leadership. Pulpit-ministers, who are usually looking for the responsive-types, sometimes cater to those with fresh enthusiasm in the fellowship. Tension and sometimes division result.

It is important for the body to grow together. The older members should be congratulated for being there. They have usually seen some trying times for the congregation. Others became discouraged and left, but they remained. No good purpose can now be served by making the older members a scapegoat for congregational ills. The "more excellent way" proposed by Paul to the bickering Corinthians was "love." That way has never been superceded.

VII

EMPOWERED BY THE SPIRIT

Power for the Task

The command of Jesus to evangelize the world is followed by the promise of his abiding Presence. "Lo, I am with you always." he told his disciples, "to the close of the age" (Matt. 28:20).

The disciples were already aware that Jesus had promised to be with them. His announcement at the Last Supper that he was leaving them filled their hearts with despair. Jesus said he would not leave them desolate. The Counselor, the Holy Spirit, would be sent by the Father in the name of Jesus (John 14:25). This Counselor would be their helper in bearing witness to Christ (John 15:27). The earthly ministry which Jesus had begun in the power of the Holy Spirit (Luke 4:14) would be continued through the Holy Spirit in the lives of those whom he had called (Acts 1:2).

After his resurrection, Jesus gave the apostles a foretaste of the power of the Spirit who would not descend in fullness until the day of Pentecost (John 20:22). Consequently, Jesus instructed the apostles to wait in Jerusalem "until you are clothed with power from on high" (Luke 24:49).

The Significance of Pentecost

The Jewish feast of Pentecost was a time of celebration for the harvest. The soil so carefully prepared and cultivated was yielding its bounty. Seed had germinated and become ripe fields of waiving grain. The one-day festival honored the Lord with the first-fruits of the harvest (Ex. 34:21-22).

Jesus at the right hand of the Father chose this festival as the time to send the Holy Spirit in his fullness (Acts 2:33). Those who came to Christ on the Day of Pentecost were to be the first fruits of a great harvest yet to come. The gospel message of forgiveness and power, first heralded on Pentecost, would be proclaimed across the centuries to millions.

Pentecost will always be remembered by Christians as the day when Christ poured out his Spirit upon the church. The enthusiasm of the apostles who had been waiting in Jerusalem for the promised Power was mistaken by the crowd for drunkenness. Peter immediately dispelled their misapprehension (Acts 2:15). This is the beginning of a new era, said Peter, when the Spirit is being given to all those who are obedient to Jesus Christ (Acts 2:17, 21, 38).

The Holy Spirit and Mission

The deep interest of the Holy Spirit in mission is reflected throughout the book of Acts. The Holy Spirit enables "sons and daughters" to "prophesy." The word "prophesy" usually requires an explanation. Many have the idea that it refers primarily to the gift of making predictions. Actually, it can often be used interchangeably in the New Testament with the idea of "preaching" or "teaching." Thus Peter announces on the day of Pentecost that even "menservants and maidservants" will be empowered by the Spirit to bear the good news to others (Acts 2:18).

Peter stood before the Sanhedrin, "filled with the Holy Spirit" (Acts 4:8). When he and John are commanded to "speak no more to any one" in the name of Jesus, he replies, "we cannot but speak what we have seen and heard" (Acts 4:20). The Holy Spirit enables the early church to continue speaking the word of God with boldness (Acts 4:31).

Because *The Acts of the Apostles* has so many references to the Spirit, this book has frequently been called *The Acts of the Holy*

Spirit. Luke often uses the word "power" and "Spirit" as synonymous. The Spirit is the power behind the mission of the church. Just as God sent forth his Son on a mission primarily to the Jews, now he sends forth the Spirit on a mission to the world.

The Spirit is always very modest. His mission is to call attention to Christ. "He will glorify me," Jesus told the apostles (John 16:14). The early church is constantly "teaching and preaching Jesus" (Acts 5:42). It is the teaching in the name of Jesus that has "filled Jerusalem" and aroused the anger of the Sanhedrin (Acts 5:28). The apostles do not preach the Spirit—they preach Christ (I Cor. 1:23), but they preach Christ in the power of the Spirit (I Cor. 2:4).

Additional references in Acts clearly point out the work of the Holy Spirit in mission. The Jews who are turning away from the salvation which Jesus came to bring are resisting the Holy Spirit (Acts 8:51). Saul of Tarsus is apprehended on the Damascus road by Christ to carry out his mission and "be filled with the Holy Spirit" (Acts 9:17). Saul and Barnabas are called by the Holy Spirit from Antioch of Syria to missionary endeavor in other fields (Acts 13:2). These references, and a number of others, all indicate the close relationship between the Spirit and the evangel.

The Divine Presence

Jesus has promised to be with his followers at all times, but in two places in the gospels, he assures his Presence in a special way. When his disciples are meeting in worship, even if the group is only two or three, "there am I," he said, "in the midst of them" (Matt. 18:20). In such an assembly, He will make the Third or Fourth.

Another time Jesus promises his Presence to his followers is when they are engaged in witnessing. The disciples are not sent out alone to evangelize. The "I am with you always" of the Great Commission has sustained his witnesses in many generations.

It is doubtful if the fear factor in evangelism can every be completely overcome. I have heard hundreds of experienced personal witnesses confess their uneasiness when they first engage a non-Christian in conversation about Christ. Even Paul confesses the "weakness' he felt when he first came to Corinth. "I was with you, he said, "in much fear and trembling" (ICor. 2:3).

The promise of power to the twelve and the seventy (Matt. 10:1; Luke 10:19) does not keep Jesus from sending them out **two by two.** Jesus undoubtedly realized the importance of human companionship. Two can lean on each other. One can be thinking and praying while the other is speaking. After talking to others about the

72

kingdom, they can compare notes in regard to the response received. It is impossible, of course, for two witnesses to be present on every occasion for personal evangelism. Sometimes it is necessary for the Christian witness to go alone. Yet he goes, with the acute consciousness that the Presence is with him.

Jesus promised the "holy" spirit to help in the work of witnessing (Acts 1:8-9). It may be assumed that there are many spirits working in the universe. The Bible also recognizes the presence of "evil" spirits as well (Matt. 12:45). Paul sees the Christian surrounded by a host of wicked spirits who are determined to stop the gospel from advancing (Eph. 6:10-12).

Henry Clay Trumbull is remembered in the history of the American Church as a vigorous advocate of the Sunday School and a great personal worker. After years of experience in talking to others about Christ, he said, "never to the present day can I speak to a single soul for Christ without being reminded by Satan that I am in danger of harming the cause by introducing it just now."

The cause of world evangelization depends upon millions of Christians finding their voices (and their hands) for Christ. Fear is often a major factor, as I have already indicated, which keeps the lips of Christians sealed. Fear leads to the determination not to witness. Once the

American church member has determined not to witness, then he looks for excuses to justify his determination. It is a frustrating cycle.

Now is the time for the Church to call attention to its mighty power. The Holy Spirit has always been available to those who engage in mission for Christ. No worker in the harvest needs to feel for one moment he is alone. The great cities of North America can be fearful places. Sometimes, even personal safety is in jeopardy. Though he should use all the physical caution possible, the Christian can still not turn away from others who need the gospel.

The Holy Spirit is the divine "energizer." He also provides strength for tired bodies and flagging wills. The American idea of "busyness" often saps energies which are needed for more vital functions. Often Christians are very tired when they go out in the community two-by-two to speak to others about Christ. In the report session which follows their visiting, I have often heard witnesses confess their reluctance to participate that evening because of weariness. Then they tell of the joy which they experiences because a family decided to accept Christ as Savior. Many students of human behavior, of course, would trace the change in their physical feelings to the stimulation of the occasion. I cannot help but believe that the Presence makes the major difference.

Power in Personal Life

The apostle Paul attaches supreme importance to the power of the Holy Spirit in personal life. He says without equivocation, "Any one who does not have the Spirit of Christ does not belong to him" (Rom. 8:9). Thus it is possible for a person to be regarded outwardly as a Christian by his contemporaries, but inwardly, God has disclaimed him.

What hinders spiritual power in the life of a Christian? Paul mentions the chasm between those who "set their minds on the things of the flesh" and "those who live according to the Spirit." (Rom. 8:5) "The mind that is set on the flesh," he continues, "is hostile to God" (Rom. 8:7).

The Christian grieves "the Holy Spirit" when his heart is filled with unforgiveness toward another person. If his mouth is filled with "evil talk" and he harbors "bitterness and wrath," then God's spirit cannot fully dwell in his life. The spirit of God wants a home in the Christian who is kind and tenderhearted (Eph. 4:29-32).

Obedience is the key to the dwelling of the Holy Spirit in the Christian life. Peter informs the Sanhedrin that he and the apostles cannot stop preaching in the name of Jesus. The forgiveness of sins through Christ must be proclaimed to all.

"We are witnesses to these things," he continued, "and so is the Holy Spirit whom God has given to those who obey him" (Acts 5:32).

The follower of Christ cannot be expected to reach spiritual maturity immediately. Time must be allowed for growth. Paul continued feeding the Corinthians on milk because they were still not ready for meat (I Cor. 8:2). The point is, however, that milk-Christians are not power-filled leaders.

Spiritual power in personal life can never be realized as long as the Christian is compromising with sin. No individual can serve God and Satan at the same time. Jesus made this truth abundantly clear (Matt. 6:24). God can use those who stumble and repent, but he will turn away from those who deliberately continue to sin (Heb. 10:26-27).

Perhaps the greatest tragedy in any century are those who limp along in their church life without real spiritual force. They may see the Holy Spirit working in others but, like Simon the Magician, they want to obtain it with worldly gifts (Acts 8:18-20). Such personal power can never be purchased merely through human resources. It is the gift which comes to those who turn over their lives completely to God (Acts 2:38).

The Vision of World Evangelization

Several times in the history of the church, Christians have caught the vision of world evangelization. Just at the time when it seems that such grand hope might be realized, the church is engulfed in an era of doubt and strife. No serious student of church history can be without some reservations in his optimism for world evangelization by the present generation.

Many students of church growth, however, are pointing to the present time as one of the great periods in evangelism. Even though some religious bodies are retrenching in membership, others are showing unprecedented growth. This is an era of church-planting when hundreds of new congregations are being born every month around the globe.

Much of the current optimism can be traced to the renewed interest of thousands in the pews of the congregations of North America. Challenged with the idea of ministry, these millions represent one of the most powerful task forces in the history of the world.

Each time the Holy Spirit moves in the hearts of the people of God, it is always with the idea of gaining new territory in the constant struggle against evil. The Spirit will not rest until "The Kingdom of the world has become the Kingdom of our Lord and of his Christ, and he shall reign for ever and ever" (Rev. 11:15).

STUDY SECTION:
TOPICS FOR DISCUSSION
NOTES

Chapter I

THE UNFULFILLED COMMISSION

1. Discuss the evidence showing Jesus intended that the gospel be preached without ethnic restrictions.

2. Give some reasons why the idea of preaching the gospel to the whole world seemed impossible.

3. What is the genius of the gospel?

4. Discuss the statement, "The New Testament makes it clear that members of a congregation have a clear-cut responsibility to live lives acceptable to Christ."

5. Do you think there is any relationship between the quality of the Christians' lives and the quantity or number of converts made?

6. List some evidences from church history that show concern for a better quality of Christian life within the congregation.

7. Comment on the statement, "A slack leadership usually results in a worldly membership."

8. Should the desire for quality in Christianity decrease the interest in quantity? Explain.

9. Why is it easy for a preaching minister to become the private chaplain to a few choice saints?

10. Do you think a concern for quantity enhances or detracts from the quality of congregational life? How?

11. How can the congregation enlarge its labor force?

12. Discuss the statement, "I cannot erase the Great Commission from my New Testament."

NOTES

Chapter II
ANALYZING THE COMMUNITY

1. What New Testament examples show that the apostles were concerned about the nature of their audience?

2. How is American society "pluralistic"?

3. Why may a congregation fail to grow even after it has all the needed information and facts about a community?

4. List some sources of information that would be helpful in making a geographical analysis of an area.

5. What is the advantage of a congregation's determining a primary geographical area for their outreach?

6. How can a map showing the congregation's area of concern be used?

7. Discuss the statement, "Social groups make up the building blocks of any society."

8. Describe the effect subcultures within an area of geographical concern may have on a congregation.

9. What is "demography"?

10. List some sources of information that would be helpful in making a demographic analysis of an area.

11. How could a demographic analysis help prevent a church from making some errors?

12. Discuss the value of making a religious analysis of a community.

NOTES

Chapter III
MAKING A WITNESS-SURVEY

1. What is the best way to find people who are living apart from the gospel?

2. Discuss some of the problems a house-to-house type of survey may present.

3. Comment on the statement, "The place to begin is with the heart of every member of the congregation."

4. Why is the typical religious census inadequate?

5. How does a witness-survey differ from the typical religious census?

6. List briefly the eight fundamental rules in conducting a witness-survey.

7. Give some of the responsibilities of the chairman of a witness-survey.

8. At what point is the average congregation most remiss concerning the witness-survey?

9. Summarize the organizing of a telephone survey that could be used for your community.

10. What are some advantages in a telephone survey?

11. Name other ways of questing that can be valuable aids in searching for those who are living apart from the gospel.

12. What relationship do you see between scheduled and spontaneous witnessing?

NOTES

Chapter IV
UNDERSTANDING THE UNCOMMITTED

1. Why is it important that the Christian seek a better understanding of the uncommitted?

2. Discuss the idea "that it is illogical to expect the uncommitted to live according to Christian ethics."

3. What are some characteristics of those in the world?

4. How has education from a purely rationalistic viewpoint influenced many Americans?

5. What mistake have Christians often made concerning those who disbelieve the Biblical claims about Christ?

6. Is the average non-Christian American probably addicted to the flesh, troubled by intellectual doubt, or simply complacent?

7. Give some Biblical teachings concerning the frailty of man.

8. Why is it important that the Christian witness be consciously aware of the basic human situation?

9. How does the gospel provide the solution to the riddle of death?

10. Comment on the statement, "The non-Christian is often unaware that the church is composed of forgiven sinners."

11. How does the divinely given idea of the congregation help meet the basic need of humans for inter-personal relationships?

12. Does man have the freedom not to choose God? Comment.

NOTES

Chapter V
GUIDELINES FOR WITNESSING

1. What is the "inadequacy-fear-syndrome"? Is it usually valid?

2. Diagram the **Witness Triangle.**

3. Why is the Acts of the Apostles an especially important book for witnessing?

4. What is usually the first step in approaching another person with the gospel?

5. List some topics one can discuss when learning about the callee.

6. Discuss the statement, "Witnessing to Christ is the apex of the gospel presentation."

7. Do most Americans have a good basic knowledge of the Bible?

8. What are some good reasons for quoting John 3:16 when witnessing for Christ?

9. Why is it true "that to miss the other person's point of view is to miss the person himself"?

10. Where is a good place to start when presenting case studies from the book of *Acts?* List some other conversion accounts from *Acts.*

11. What is the worst mistake of all in Christian witnessing?

12. What matters would you discuss concerning the future of the new convert?

NOTES

Chapter VI
CALLED TO MINISTER

1. Do you think the most crucial time in the life of a new Christian is the first few months? Explain.

2. What disciplines can one expect as a Christian?

3. Should new Christians be discouraged from being enthusiastic witnesses? Comment.

4. Discuss some goals you think your congregation should strive to meet.

5. How has the mobility of American society influenced our congregations?

6. Comment on the statement, "All Christians need a group of believers to whom they can relate on a primary basis."

7. What error has been frequently made in the educating of pulpit-ministers?

8. Do you agree that "every Christian is a minister of Jesus Christ"? Explain.

9. What problems may be encountered when an effort is made to train the laity for ministering?

10. What are the mini-type colleges?

11. Why are there sometimes conflicts between newer and older members of a congregation?

12. How should one deal with the above conflicts?

NOTES

Chapter VII
EMPOWERED BY THE SPIRIT

1. How were the disciples to be empowered for their God-given tasks?

2. Discuss the significance of God's choosing the Jewish feast of Pentecost to the fulfillment of Christ's promise to send the Holy Spirit.

3. Comment on the statement, "The Spirit is the power behind the mission of the church."

4. Is there any relationship between resisting the Holy Spirit and rejecting Christ? Explain.

5. Name two instances in which Jesus promises His presence with the disciples in a special way.

6. Do you think the evil spirits attempt to keep Christians from witnessing? How?

7. Can a person be a Christian and not have the Holy Spirit?

8. What are some things that grieve the Holy Spirit?

9. What is the key to the dwelling of the Holy Spirit in the Christian's life?

10. How are some people today like Simon the Magician?

11. Give some reasons why many students of church growth are cautiously optimistic today.

12. When will the Holy Spirit rest?

NOTES

APPENDIX
HOW TO CONDUCT A SCHOOL OF EVANGELISM
SAMPLE CENSUS CARD

HOW TO CONDUCT A SCHOOL OF EVANGELISM

Evangelism in America is frequently left in the hands of "professionals." In a School of Evangelism, a direct challenge is given to the people in the pews to be evangelists for Christ. Consequently, the New Testament concept of the ministry of all believers with every Christian an evangelist is brought more sharply into focus (Act 8:4).

Vertical Services

In Schools of Evangelism which I conduct, I find it possible to gather more people on a Sunday for four services than to try using four week nights. Circumstances vary, however, in different communities. It may be best in some areas to conduct the School on two consecutive Sundays. These services include the Sunday morning Bible School hour, the morning worship service, a second Bible School session in the evening, and a Sunday night "Care-Promise" service. (See resource section.)

Morning Bible School Session

A combined class in the church sanctuary of all those from the high school class up through the adult classes usually begins the School. A preaching minister should probably conduct the class. In a congregation with more than one person on the preaching staff, the minister of evangelism would be the logical leader. In some congregations, a leader with the "heart of an evangelist" could serve.

I devote the morning Bible School session to two basic principles of church growth: (1) the principle of gathering and scattering and (2) the principle of the taught teaching. Material for these principles and their explanation may be found in *The Growing Congregation* (Lincoln, Illinois: LCC Press). Allow some time for discussion, but try to save most of the discussion for the evening Bible School session.

The leader may decide to weave in information from the scheduled lesson, or suggest that each "save" that information for the next Sunday and combine it with the lesson for that day.

Morning Worship Service

Select hymns which call attention to the harvest (Matt. 9:36-38). These songs are listed in the hymnal under topics such as "Soul Winning," "Mission," or "Evangelism." An anthem or special number on the same theme can be very effective.

Whereas the primary purpose of the Bible School lesson is instruction, the controlling idea of the morning sermon should be motivation. I may intellectually accept the idea that the Great Commission is given to every Christian and still sit in the pew every Sunday morning and not be a Christian witness. My heart must be stirred. I must care enough to act.

Second Bible School Session

This class is a *continuation* of the morning Bible School. Allow plenty of time for discussion. Discuss the reasons "why" the average person who sits in a pew on Sunday morning is not a witness. Deal with the basic problem of fear which most people have regarding personal evangelism. Also deal with the problem of finding the time. You may want to utilize the section, "Suggestions for Planned Harvesting for Christ," in *The Growing Congregation.*

Using the "Care-Promise" Card

In each of the four services, call attention to the "Care-Promise" idea. Point out that it is easier to give money to help others be missionaries than it is to be witnesses for Christ ourselves. (See the resources section for additional information.)

The Harvest Choir

The addition of a "Harvest Choir" for the evening service stimulates interest and enthusiasm. This choir is composed of the regular choir members plus additional singers recruited especially for the School of Evangelism. Usually, the second Bible School session begins an hour and a half before the time of the evening commitment service. The Harvest Choir rehearses a half-hour before evening services begin. Participants in the choir who are in the second Bible School have received most of the information and are excused for rehearsal. Someone should be appointed to be in charge of recruiting the Harvest Choir. Do not overlook the young people.

Sunday Evening[1] Care-Promise Service

Once again, songs should be chosen which follow the theme of soul winning. At the close of the evening message (before the "invitation hymn"), someone in the congregation who is known for his concern for the lost usually takes the lead in the Care-Promise service. He reminds the congregation once again that every Christian is an evangelist. I suggest the following steps:

1. Have the ushers pass out the Care-Promise cards. (They should have these ready before the service begins.)

2. Ask the people not to write on the cards until instructed.

3. Read the card and its Scripture and give a brief word of encouragement.

[1] I recognize that many congregations do not have Sunday evening services. In that case, I recommend either using two Sunday mornings for a School of Evangelism or scheduling a "special" Sunday evening service.

4. Have someone from the congregation posted to lead in a prayer of dedication. Let the people remain seated.

5. Ask the people to fill in the card. A twelve-month period is suggested.

6. Collect the cards.

NOTE: The ushers should already be instructed to make two tallies: (1) The number to be won; (2) The number from the congregation who are participating. These numbers are announced just prior to the closing chorus.

Prayer Circles

While the ushers are completing the tallies, divide the congregation into groups of 12 and form prayer circles. This idea is a familiar one to young people who have attended Christian service camps. Many of the adults, however, have never participated in a prayer circle.

Choose enough prayer leaders so that each group of 12 has a leader. Often the officers are the logical ones to lead. Another way to obtain leaders is to let that person lead the group whose birthday is closest to the date. Prayers are to be directed toward the harvest of souls and the compelling need for more harvesters (Matthew 9:38).

After one of the ushers announces the tallies, the one directing the music leads out in a closing chorus. An announcement should be made that anyone desiring to come to Christ that evening should come then.

Follow-Up

Those who have participated in the Care-Promise commitment should be contacted and instructed for calling. Choose a week night (perhaps Wednesday) or Saturday afternoon. Team up experienced callers with new callers. Sometimes three people can form a team.

Take the new callers through *How in the World?* and keep helping them in actual witnessing.

RESOURCES

The Care-Promise Commitment

Many congregations today are familiar with the **Faith-Promise** concept in missionary giving. A definite goal is established. Following a period of inspiration and instruction, members of the congregation are given an opportunity to commit a part of their income to global missions. Some churches have revolutionized their missionary giving through the **Faith-Promise** idea.

The **Care-Promise** idea works in a similar way. Members of the congregation are asked to commit their lives to the winning of others to Jesus Christ. Some congregations have been revoiutionized in church growth through the **Care-Promise** commitment. Following a period of teaching and motivation sometimes called "A School of Evangelism," Christians are asked to commit themselves to a definite goal in soul winning. The emphasis throughout is upon the idea of every Christian an evangelist.

Below is a sample commitment card:

" . . . The harvest is plentiful, but the laborers are few;

CARE-PROMISE

Because I care, I promise to try with God's help to win
_____ *people to Christ during the next* _____ *months.*

Name _____

Date _____

. . . pray therefore the Lord of the harvest to send out laborers into his harvest."   —Matt. 9:37, 38

Care-Promise cards are available in quantities of 100 at $1.75 from either Standard Publishing, 8121 Hamilton Avenue, Cincinnati, Ohio 45231. or LCC Bookstore, Box 178, Lincoln, Illinois 62656. Also Care-Promise bulletins and posters are available from the same addresses. Write for samples and prices.

Advance News Release Sent to Newspapers
Two Weeks Prior to the School of Evangelism

Name and Address of Congregation
Name and Telephone of contact person in con-
gregation
Date

The _____(name)_____ Church is
planning for a School of Evangelism on
_____(date)_____. These special services
will be led by _____(name and position)_____.

The purpose of the School of Evangelism is to
encourage every member of the congregation to
be a personal evangelist for Jesus Christ.
Realizing that three out of every four homes in
America and Canada are a mission field, the
leaders of the _____(name)_____ Church are ready to
show their concern.
many new people they will personally try to
bring to Christ during the next year.

The services being planned are:
First Bible School session   (time)
Morning worship service   (time)
Second Bible School session   (time)
Evening worship service   (time)
The evening service will close with a Care-
Promise Service where members of the con-
gregation will be requested to indicate how

Follow-Up News Release
(Immediately following School of Evangelism)

Name and Address of Congregation
Name and Telephone of contact person in congregation
Date

During a School of Evangelism conducted recently at the _____ Church, ____(address)____, _____ members of the congregation promised to try, with God's help, to win _____ new people to Christ during the next year.

The School of Evangelism began at the Sunday morning Bible School and continued through the day. In the evening service. a Care-Promise Service was led by _____. A challenge was given to each member to become a personal witness for Jesus Christ and share his faith with others in the community.

At the close of the evening service, members of the congregation gathered in prayer circles to ask God's help as they seek to become evangelists for him. Those who have not participated in evangelistic calling before will be sent out with experienced callers.

The _____ Church seeks to serve its community by bringing the gospel of

Christ to every unchurched person in the area. A special emphasis will be made upon Sunday School classes for the children of the community.

Members of the _____ Church will be grateful for the prayers and concern of the people in this community.

SAMPLE CENSUS CARD

ADDRESS _____ floor _____
(street number)   (city or suburb)   apt. _____

DATE _____ Not Home ☐ Vacant ☐ Refused ☐ Other ☐

First Name	Mem-ber	At-tends	Pre-fers	List specific church & community
Mr. _____	☐	☐	☐	_____
Mrs. _____	☐	☐	☐	_____
Other _____	☐	☐	☐	_____

No. of Children _____   Names   Name of Sunday School

Sunday ⎰ Pre-School   1-5   _____   _____
School ⎱ Grades   6-14   _____   _____
         High School 15-18 _____   _____

Where attending now _____
                          (church)   (location)

Adults attend : Regularly ____ Occasionally ____ Seldom ____ Never ____
Children attend: Regularly ____ Occasionally ____ Seldom ____ Never ____

FAMILY NAME _____ phone _____

Use other side of card for special information

106

REFERENCES AND COMMENTS

INTRODUCTION

The student of American Church Growth can be grateful for the abundance of materials in evangelism now coming from the presses. We have just passed through a "dry period" when very little on evangelism was being published.

Contributing to the flow of evangelistic materials is the emphasis of Key 73. The *Key 73 Congregational Resource Book* probably represents the first attempt in the history of the American Church to bring together such a wide variety of tools and resources in church growth.

The shift in emphasis in evangelism today is clearly toward the congregation. The local church has often been maligned in previous years because the average congregation appeared so spiritually anemic. Most churches seemed too "lame, same, and tame" to evangelize.

Now, many congregations are pulsating with new life. Young people who previously had to look for genuine Christian fellowship outside the traditional church are finding a new openness of congregational leaders. People attending large evangelistic crusades are asking, "Why can't we have this same kind of spirit in our church?"

The reader who may be inclined to be critical of some of the resource material which will be listed in this section should be aware that I may not necessarily agree with all the conclusions of the authors. In fact, I may even reject their basic presuppositions. They are listed as reading support for a particular chapter because I feel their writings lend insight. Some of the books are more suitable for advanced students who are doing extensive research in church growth.

CHAPTER I

I am indebted to the article on the "Great Commission" in Hasting's *A Dictionary of Christ and the Gospels* for the summaries of the Commissions. This is an older work but still very useful. I have made a few slight changes in the wording of the diagram.

CONTENTS OF COMMISSION COMMON TO EVANGELISTS			
Matt. 28:18-10	Mark 16:14-18	Luke 24:46-49	John 20:21-23
Universal Mission	Universal Mission	Universal Mission	Mission of undefined range
Teaching Baptism Teaching	Faith and Baptism	Repentance and Remission of sins	Forgiveness
Promise of spiritual Presence	Signs to accompany those who believe	Promise of Comforter	Gift of Holy Spirit

The student should be aware of the textual problems in the "long ending" of Mark. Further discussion may be found in a good commentary. Also he should realize that the tendency today in New Testament studies is to completely separate the witness of John from the synoptics.

The serious student of church growth will not want to overlook Adolph Harnack. *The Mission and Expansion of Christianity in the First Three Centuries* (Harper Torchbook) or Michael Green, *Evangelism in the Early Church* (Eerdmans). Harnack's arguments against a universal commission are implausible, I feel, on a textual basis. In these studies, one may catch in a remarkable way the significance of the congregation in the growth of early Christianity. My book, *The Growing Congregation* (LCC Press), is an abbreviated study of the congregation in the New Testament. *Body Life* (GIL Publications) by Ray C. Stedman is a helpful study about the "quality" of congregational life. Also, *How Churches Grow* and *Understanding Church Growth* by Donald A. McGavran are extremely valuable. Both of these books are having amazing influence all across America. A Festschrift in honor of Dr. McGavran entitled *God, Man and Church Growth* (Eerdmans) and edited by A. R. Tippett should be studied by those interested in American Church Growth.

CHAPTER II

This chapter appeared originally in the *Church Growth Manual* printed by Standard Publishing in 1969. I have rewritten the article and used it for this section. My gratitude is expressed to Dr. Ralph M. Small, Vice-President and Publisher, who gave me the permission to use it.

I must also express my indebtedness to the excellent study by Charles S. Mueller, *The Strategy of Evangelism* (Concordia). I have utilized his population pyramid. In Lincoln Christian Seminary, we have used this book as collateral reading for courses in church growth for several years.

One of the best books I have come across on the situation of the changing neighborhood is *The Church in the Racially Changing Community* (Abingdon) by Robert L. Wilson and James H. Davis. Although we are further down the road of "two cultures" in America than we were in 1966, this book still contains many useful insights.

It is of great sadness to me that the black and white communities seem to be moving further apart. Only the gospel, I feel, can bridge the gap. Many attempts at the integrated church have failed, but there are places where it is working. These congregations should be carefully studied. One of the great experiences in our family life is the opportunity to worship on many occasions with   black congregation. I hold with others the view that some of the greatest preaching in America is taking place in the black community.

CHAPTERS III & V

Since these chapters are so closely related, I am dealing with them here as a unit.

I have felt that the typical religious census has needed improvement for a long time. The idea of a "witness-survey" occurred to me several years ago. Others have evidently had similar feelings to mine, because I am seeing the "personal approach" in many survey materials.

I served for several years on the Congregational Task Force for Key 73. Part of our committee responsibility was to read the materials being produced by religious groups in America in their departments of evangelism. I systematically began to read one program after another. Some of the material in this book reflects my research in this area of study.

Resource materials for these two chapters may be found by turning to Phase Three of the *Key 73 Congregational Resource Book* and the Bibliography. Additional helps for these chapters are: Joe Ellis, *The Personal Evangelist*

(Standard); *Meet My Savior* (Beacon Hill Press); Wilfred Lown, *What Do You Think?* (Manhattan Christian College: Manhattan, Kansas); *Go!* (Light and Life) William A. Powell, *Church Bus Evangelism* (P. O. Box 3428, Orlando, Florida); and James H. Jauncey, *Psychology for Successful Evangelism* (Moody). Virgil Gerber's; *A Manual for Evangelism/Church Growth* (William Carey) is a very useful tool for plotting the congregational rate of church growth and making projections for the future.

Americans who have serious doubts about the Bible can catch another point of view by reading A. M. Hunter, *The Unity of the New Testament* (SCM Press); Bernard Ramm, *The Christian View of Science and the Scripture* (Eerdmans); A. Leonard Griffith, *Barriers to Christian Belief* (Harper); and David A. Hubbard, *Does the Bible Really Work?* (Word).

The works of C. S. Lewis are among the best apologies for Christianity. (See in particular *Miracles, The Problem of Pain, The Weight of Glory, God in the Dock, Christian Reflections).* C. E. M. Joad and his works are also very valuable (see *The Recovery of Belief,* Hillary). The New Testament itself, of course, is the best apology of all (John 20:30-31). Many people who severely criticize the gospel have never bothered to read the New Testament. The

Evangelical Reprint Library by College Press, Joplin, Missouri, has many fine studies of an apologetic nature.

CHAPTER IV

The study of man has been a consuming interest for philosophers and theologians for many years. A list of some of the important studies in this field are as follows: Martin Buber, *I and Thou* (The Scribner Library) and "What Is Man?" an essay in his book *Between Man and Man* (Macmillan). I especially appreciate reading *The Destiny of Man* (Harper Torchbook) by Nicholas Berdyaev. Paul Tillich in Volume II of his *Systematic Theology* (Chicago) deals with man's estrangement. H. Richard Niebuhr in *The Responsible Self* (Harper) seeks to find a basis for man's moral life. G. K. Chesterton's *Everlasting Man* (Hodder and Stoughton) is also of value.

In the last century, Immanuel Kant with his *Religion Within the Limits of Reason Alone* (Harper Torchbook) probes the conflict of the good with the evil in man. Friedrich Schleiermacher in *The Christian Faith* (II Volumes, Harper Torchbook) gives an analysis of man's religious self-consciousness. Both Calvin and Luther are intensely interested in man. Thomas Acquinas has a "Treatise on Man" in Part I, Questions 75-112, of the *Summa.*

From a Christian perspective, the final authority regarding the nature of man is the Bible. For this reason, I have limited myself largely in this chapter to quotations from scripture. At the same time, it is surely unwise to ignore what some of the most thoughtful writers across the centuries have said on the nature of man.

CHAPTER VI

The idea of equipping all Christians to be ministers of Jesus Christ is gaining wider and wider acceptance in the American Church. One of the leading spokesmen in this area is Dr. Earl C. Hargrove (see page 51ff of *The Preachers Are Coming,* LCC Press). A task force in evangelism of millions of American Christians is well within sight. Here is a force combined with other Christians of other continents which can revolutionize the world.

Again I would refer the reader to the Bibliography of the *Key 73 Congregational Resource Book.* Supplementary study should also include Yves Congar, *Lay People in the Church* (Christian Classics), and *The Layman in Christian History* (Westminster) edited by Neill and Weber.

New Testament Follow-Up (Eerdmans) by Waylon B. Moore and *Let Yourself Grow* (Standard) by Joe Ellis also give some very practical help toward helping new Christians develop in the faith.

It is important that congregations have a good system of keeping records. Most publishing houses furnish samples. You may also write to Church Data Consultant, 15404 South Prairie Avenue, Lawndale, California 90260.

CHAPTER VII

The latter part of the twentieth century is being referred to by an increasing number of writers as "the age of the Holy Spirit." Whether this designation is more appropriate today than in other periods of church history, I would be reluctant to say. I do know that religious writing today reflects a tremendous interest in the work of the Holy Spirit.

Some of the writers in previous generations also had a deep interest in the Holy Spirit. An older work by Robert Richardson entitled *Office of the Holy Spirit* is very valuable. H. B. Swete, the English classical scholar, was deeply concerned about the Holy Spirit. Recently reprinted by Baker is his *The Holy Spirit in the New Testament,* containing a special section on "the gift of tongues."

A contemporary theologian whose writings contribute heavily to the study of the Holy Spirit is Karl Barth. The subject keeps recurring in his *Church Dogmatics.* Although he discusses the Holy Spirit in Volume I, his fullest treatment comes in Volume IV when he is dealing with "The Doctrine of Reconciliation." Editor Harold Lindsell recently contributed a major article in Christianity Today entitled "Tests for the Tongues Movement" (December 8, 1972, pp. 240-244).

Those who want additional information on the day of Pentecost from the standpoint of a Jewish feast are encouraged to consult the three-volume set in *Judaism* (Harvard University Press) by George Foot Moore.

A work which I have consulted continually while writing the Biblical sections of this book is the multi-volume Theological Dictionary of the New Testament (Eerdmans). Here is a gold mine of information for those who have some background in the original languages.

The quotation from Trumbull may be found in his *Individual Work by Individuals* (American Tract Society), pages 168-169.

Paul Benjamin is a professor in the Departments of New Testament and Church Growth in Lincoln Christian Seminary, a member of the Executive Committee of Key 73, and the newly appointed director of *National Church Growth Research Center* in Washington, D. C.

He was educated at Lincoln Christian College, Butler University, Northern Baptist Theological Seminary, and the University of Iowa. He holds the Doctor of Theology in New Testament and has completed two years of post-doctoral work in special studies relating to American Church Growth.